RELIGIOUS AND MORAL EDUCATION PRESS

Religious and Moral Education Press
An imprint of Chanistor Publications Ltd,
a wholly owned subsidiary of Hymns Ancient & Modern Ltd
St Mary's Works, St Mary's Plain
Norwich, Norfolk NR3 3BH

First published 1996
Reprinted 1997

ISBN 1–85175–110–6

Acknowledgements
Biblical extracts are from the New English Bible, © Oxford University Press and Cambridge University Press 1961, 1970, and are used by permission.

The extract from *Winnie-the-Pooh*, by A. A. Milne (Methuen), is reproduced by permission of Reed Books.

The extract from 'Harvest Home', by John Betjeman, from his *Collected Poems*, is reproduced by permission of John Murray (Publishers) Ltd.

The words of 'When I Needed a Neighbour', by Sidney Carter, are reproduced by permission of Stainer & Bell Ltd.

Every effort has been made to contact copyright owners and the author and publisher apologize to any whose rights have inadvertently not been acknowledged.

Designed and typeset by *T*opics – *The Creative Partnership*, Exeter
Printed in Great Britain by Unwin Brothers Ltd, Old Woking, Surrey for Chanistor Publications Ltd, Norwich

Contents

••

Introduction

There is a general acceptance amongst teachers, governors and parents that school assemblies have an important role to play in the overall provision a school makes for the moral, spiritual and religious education of its students, and that good assemblies contribute to the ethos and sense of identity that a school wishes to promote. There is far less agreement about the format, style and content of assemblies, their frequency, and the grouping of students for them.

Although they are often used for other purposes as well, assemblies normally incorporate the required act of collective worship, and the debate about the meaning of 'broadly Christian' will continue. In most schools, the pattern and nature of assemblies and collective worship have been determined by tradition, by the availability of suitable premises, and through discussions on the provision of what seems to be most appropriate in the particular context of the school. Those who have responsibilities for taking assemblies and collective worship, and students and teachers who – willingly or unwillingly – attend, are likely to agree that it is the quality of the overall experiences derived from assemblies and acts of collective worship that will determine their success or otherwise and their contribution to the development of young people. One key to success is the quality of the theme chosen for the collective worship part of the assembly and the way in which it is developed. The aim of this book, therefore, is to provide some suitable material for those leading assemblies.

I have taken assemblies for nearly thirty years. In earlier years, most were year or form assemblies with relatively small groups of children of similar age in a Grammar school in Berkshire. Later, as a Head of House in a Comprehensive school serving a new development area on the edge of the Birmingham conurbation, I gave assemblies to the very diverse group of students that made up the House. Promotion to Deputy Head took me to a large Comprehensive school on the east coast; the premises did not allow the whole school to assemble in one place, and my assemblies were usually given to year groups, or, once a week, to either the Lower School (Years 7 to 9) or the Upper School (Years 10 to 13).

Then, for over ten years until December 1994, I was Head of a large Comprehensive school in Nottinghamshire. Each Friday morning, well over 1000 students from Year 7 to Year 13 and all staff gathered in the sports hall in perfect order for the weekly full school assembly. Other gatherings took place on other days in much smaller groupings; it would have been counter-productive and logistically very difficult to have had a full school assembly more frequently, but we were able to do so very successfully once a week, and I regarded it as one of the most important regular events in the life of the school. The combination of a more formal weekly full-school assembly and more intimate House assemblies suited our circumstances and ethos well; other, completely different, arrangements suit different schools equally successfully. The common factors in all schools should be the care and thought that are put into all assemblies so that, in their own particular way, they contribute to the overall aims of the school.

Each section of the book is based on an assembly or assemblies I have taken. The majority have been for full-school assemblies, though many have also been used as the basis of other assemblies in various places over the years. The best assemblies are usually those which are topical or have a personal association for the person taking the assembly – speaking from personal knowledge or belief provides greater conviction. Many sections of this book are based on my personal experiences, but the content is presented in an impersonal way so that it can be used in whatever form is felt appropriate. Although some of my best assemblies have been based on personal experiences, I have also relied heavily for large numbers of assemblies on other sources. Most of us have neither the time nor the inspiration to produce our own original material every time. I have been most grateful to numerous people who have given me ideas and thoughts for entire assemblies or for parts of assemblies. Many of their books and articles are readily available, but I hope that this book will add to the range of source material that can be drawn on by those who wish to provide high quality, relevant assemblies, without spending a disproportionate amount of time on preparation.

The book can be used in many ways depending on the requirements of the school. An assembly could be used as a complete freestanding item, or it might be a reading as part of a broader theme. One of these assemblies could be the basis of notes for your own assembly which are then personalized and elaborated as necessary. Other activities, such as music or drama, can be incorporated according to the traditions and needs of the school; some of the longer assemblies might possibly be used as the basis of two consecutive assemblies.

Each assembly is written so that it can be delivered as a whole by one person. Of course, additional material, including music and visual aids, can often be used, and alternative ways of delivery may be more appropriate, particularly when smaller numbers of students are gathered together and the opportunities for their active involvement are greater. Some suggestions for possible alternative ways of presentation are given at the beginning of each assembly. The assemblies are grouped into thematic sections and the title of each assembly gives an indication of its theme and content. Some of the ideas, themes and subject matters that are developed are shown by a few key words or phrases at the beginning of each assembly. In addition, the thematic index will help those who wish to explore a particular theme in one or more assemblies.

The book is not specifically 'religious' or Christian, although biblical and other religious readings are used. Its themes are essentially moral ones which are generally accepted by people of good will from all religions or none. Many of the issues that are covered are complex. I make no apology for this as I believe it is important to challenge and stimulate young people, and bland platitudes have no place on occasions when the school ethos is being positively promoted. However, at a large gathering and with limited time, discussion of the issues is not possible as a rule, but there will usually be opportunities for detailed discussions to take place in time set aside for Personal and Social Education and similar activities; the book could be used to provide useful source material for such classes. A short prayer is included with each section; it usually invokes an Almighty God rather than containing a reference to a particular religious tradition. The prayer can, of course, be left out or be modified as appropriate for the particular school.

Further perspectives – Christian or other – can be incorporated into the theme of each assembly as needed. Although from a Christian background myself, I have always believed strongly that assemblies should be inclusive rather than exclusive, and I have taken pride in the fact that no student or member of staff ever 'opted out' of the assemblies I provided. I believe it is very important for assemblies to be truly corporate and to emphasize universal values, such as honesty, commitment, service, integrity, courtesy, consideration, co-operation and respect, which are fundamental principles of Christianity and other faiths, and many moral codes. I hope that those who have the very significant and demanding responsibility of leading many different sorts of assemblies in different contexts will find this book useful.

IAN STUART
1996

Dedication
To the pupils, students and staff of Grove School, Balderton, Newark, Nottinghamshire

1

Personal Qualities

Advice to Young People

* Knowing yourself
* Achieving self-knowledge through challenges
* Learning humility
* Our dependence on the past and on others
* Seeking the truth
* Idealism of youth

The introduction – along the lines of the first paragraph – could be given by a pupil who then invites three adults to offer suggestions of advice on what to do. Three adults, in turn, would either read or talk about each of the three suggestions. The leader could then sum up the suggestions, and introduce the reading, read by the pupil who introduced the assembly.

Young people sometimes complain that adults, and teachers in particular, are always telling them what not to do, rather than suggesting what to do. The criticism is often justified, so here is some advice on what to do, concentrating on three topics.

First, **'know yourself'**. You are the one person you will have to live with for the rest of your life. Failure to understand the strengths and weaknesses of your own personality means that you will be living with a stranger. It's more than that: if you don't know yourself, how can you form genuine relationships or friendships with others? If you don't know yourself, how can you cope with the problems in life?

But knowing yourself is not easy. How can you attempt it? Some communities of monks insist that at times each monk spends a week entirely alone in a cell; the idea is that in this time the monk will remove the 'cotton-wool' around himself and discover his true self. This is a bit drastic and not possible for most people, but the need for some time and space to yourself is important. Others say that we understand our true selves only when we face challenges. There is much in this; certainly we need challenges – mental and physical – to discover our strengths and weaknesses. There are many ways to encounter challenges: for instance, schemes like the Duke of Edinburgh Award Scheme or courses run by organizations such as the Outward Bound Trust can provide valuable experiences for young people.

Whatever path you choose, you will find self-knowledge is achieved only after a long, hard struggle. But don't give up, as some do, and seek escape through drink, drugs or cheap pleasures.

Secondly, **'learn humility'**. Humility is a rather old-fashioned word but its use helps us to avoid thinking that we are too important. You are, of course, unique. But you are only a tiny part of history. Although we rightly stress the importance of the individual, we are all dependent on each other. We are also dependent on the past, and those who will come in the future will be dependent on us. You do not have a free hand to do what you want regardless of the past and regardless of the future. Be proud of the achievements of the human race, but remember that we are not at the top of humankind's achievements: we are only at one point in time in the evolution of the human race.

Thirdly, **'seek the truth'**. This sounds simple, but it isn't. The truth is always very complex. We are too used to the easy answers of newspapers, television and other mass opinion formers today; advertisements constantly telling us that their products are best devalue the meaning of truth. If we want the truth, there is no substitute for hard work and hard thinking. If the truth is ugly, face it; if it is beautiful, don't sneer at it. The truth, in all its complexity, will never be easy to find.

So, here are three suggestions of what to do:

Know yourself – you will have to live with yourself for the rest of your life.

•••••••••• CHALLENGES FOR LIVING ••••••••••

Learn humility – although unique, you are only a tiny particle at this particular time in history.

Seek the truth – this is often difficult, but without the truth nothing is real.

This short reading suggests that the ideals that young people have, such as truth, are the possessions that bring real wealth. The reading is taken from a book by Albert Schweitzer, a famous medical missionary and philosopher, who devoted much of his life from 1913 to his death in 1965, to a medical mission in Africa. Though there has been criticism of some aspects of his life, his contribution in this field is undisputed. He was awarded the Nobel Peace prize in 1952.

Grown-up people reconcile themselves too willingly to a supposed duty of preparing young ones for a time when they will regard as illusion what is now an inspiration to heart and mind. It is through the idealism of youth that people catch sight of truth, and in that idealism they possess a wealth that they must never exchange for anything else. Grow into your ideals so that life can never rob you of them.

At the present time when violence, clothed in life, dominates the world more cruelly than it ever has before, I still remain convinced that truth, love, peaceableness, meekness, and kindness are the violence that can master all other violence.

(from *Memoirs of Youth*, slightly adapted)

A PRAYER FOR HUMAN UNDERSTANDING

O God, give us thoughtfulness, imagination and patience to discover why other people feel and think and behave as they do, so that our understanding may grow and our sympathy may deepen. Show us how to use our insight to help our friends, our companions and our enemies.

Amen.

Using Our Potential

* ❋ Envy and jealousy of others
* ❋ Realizing our potential
* ❋ Using what we have and striving to develop ourselves

There is a well-known folk story that many people will remember, but it is worth telling again because it helps to illustrate some interesting characteristics of the behaviour of many human beings.

This is the story of a girl who lived on a farm high up on a hillside. Every morning she looked out of her bedroom window across the valley to a hill on the far side. On this hill was a house with golden windows. She longed to see this house. She thought that it must be a marvellous place, and she wished that she lived there instead of in her own house which was very ordinary.

One morning she made up her mind that she was going to see that house for herself. She set off, but the journey turned out to be much longer than she had expected. It was already getting dark when she eventually got near to the house on the other hillside. And you can imagine how disappointed she was when she saw that the windows were not golden, but just like those of her own house.

It was now too late to go back, so she knocked on the door of the house and an old lady opened it. The girl told her story to the old lady, who invited her in and introduced the girl to her husband. They gave her a meal, and later on the girl went to bed. The next day she woke to a morning of glorious sunshine. She looked out of her window and across the valley she saw her own house ...

Yes, you've guessed! The sun was shining on her house and it had golden windows! She was glad to get back to her own lovely home.

It is easy to think that what others have is better, whether it is a house, a family, good looks, brains or anything else. There is an old

Personal Qualities

saying, 'The grass is always greener on the other side'. It is really making the same point as the story – that it is easy to imagine that life is better elsewhere. But in reality it depends on how we look at things. We may well envy some of our friends, or anyone else for that matter, for who they are or what they have, but it may be that they envy us and what we have. What we must do is to move beyond that: instead of envying each other or being jealous of what others have, we must strive to do better in our own lives and to achieve better things.

The human race has survived only because people have improved themselves and have sought to develop themselves. The real secret of life is to make the best of what we have – our brains, our fitness, our skills, our personalities, everything that is part of us. Often we don't realize just how much we have; sadly, it may only be when we lose something – or, worse, when we lose someone – that we realize what we have lost.

All of us have the possibility of doing a tremendous amount. The word 'potential' is used to describe what is possible but has not yet been realized. We all have potential, and much of it may be hidden and unused as yet. We need to look for the key to unlock our potential so that it can be used for our own benefit and for the benefit of others. If this happens then, indeed, the human race will continue to develop.

Don't be envious of others. We may think that they have more than we have or that they have a better life; we may think that their house has golden windows. But we all have much to offer – usually far more than we realize. We need to use it for the fulfilment of our lives and for the benefit of our world.

A PRAYER

O God, we ask for help not only to be content with what we have, but to be able to use what we have to the best advantage. We pray that we may seek ways to develop our potential to improve ourselves for the benefit of the whole human race.

Amen.

Success despite Difficulties

* Using opportunities and talents
* Being positive
* The example of Alexander Murray
* What is success?

A map of Scotland would enable Galloway to be pin-pointed. Murray's Monument is close to the A712 between New Galloway and Newton Stewart.

The south-west corner of Scotland is called Galloway. It is a relatively small area of coast and mountain, forest and moorland, river and lake (or loch, to use the Scottish word). Its remote and unspoiled location makes it a lovely place for a holiday.

In this area, on top of a steep hill, is a huge monument made from great blocks of granite. It is called Murray's Monument and was erected over a hundred years ago to the memory of a man who was born in a remote cottage near this spot. Who was this man to whom the monument was erected?

Alexander Murray was born about the year 1800 in an isolated shepherd's cottage, several miles from the nearest neighbour and accessible only by the roughest of tracks. The only possible occupation for anyone there was looking after sheep. Imagine then the despair of Alexander's parents upon the discovery, when he was six, that he was so shortsighted that he couldn't tell the difference between a sheep and a rock. What sort of shepherd would he make?

Proper schooling for him was out of the question, but Alexander soon learned to read, and he read everything he could get hold of. He then became interested in learning European languages. His fame spread, and by the age of eighteen he was much in demand as a tutor. He went to Edinburgh University and turned his attention to the languages of the East – Chinese, Japanese, Malayan, and others, and soon after his thirtieth birthday, he was appointed Professor of Oriental

Personal Qualities

15

Languages at Edinburgh University. He is still remembered today as one of Scotland's most distinguished professors.

What is there in this story for us? It is not that we should all try to become Professor of Oriental Languages at Edinburgh University! Alexander Murray was obviously a genius, but he succeeded without the benefits we would consider essential for success, and in the face of enormous difficulties. We are ordinary people, but we have so many advantages at our disposal. Of course, life has, and will always have, its difficulties, some of them very great, but the message of the story of Alexander Murray is simple: use your opportunities to the full. Success will be measured in different ways for different people, but the key to success is to use your opportunities fully. It is sad to see people being negative rather than positive and letting opportunities slip away. The story of Alexander Murray – who succeeded in the face of enormous difficulties – is an encouragement to everyone to live life to the full and to take maximum advantage of the opportunities presented.

This short extract, written over a hundred years ago, is about success:

A person has achieved success who has lived well, laughed often, and loved much; who has gained the respect of intelligent people and the love of little children; who has filled their niche and accomplished their task; who has left the world better than they found it, whether by an improved poppy, a perfect poem, or a rescued soul; who never lacked appreciation of earth's beauty or failed to express it; who has looked for the best in others and given the best they had; whose life was an inspiration; whose memory is a benediction.

(A. P. Stanley, 1815–81, adapted)

A PRAYER

✵

O God, help us not to waste or hide our talents. Draw out from each of us the capabilities that have been planted in us; help us to use them all in the service of our fellow people.

Amen.

Courage

* The dangers of the sea and the work of the R.N.L.I. and other rescue services
* Grace Darling and her bravery
* Faith in God and belief in a purpose in life

Although about courage and faith generally, this assembly is particularly associated with the sea, and could be linked with R.N.L.I. flag days. The hymn 'Eternal Father strong to save' could be sung or a recording of it played. Other music that has connections with the sea, such as Mendelssohn's 'Hebrides' Overture, would be appropriate as an introduction or a conclusion to the assembly. The reading could be read by a pupil.

Britain is surrounded by the sea, so it is not surprising that the sea has played a very significant part in the history of these islands – as a means of transport, as a source of food and as a dominant influence in the lives of many people who live or work on or near the sea. All who know the sea are well aware of its power and treat it with respect. Over the centuries, many lives have been lost in shipwrecks, and our history is full of examples of the heroism of people who have shown great courage in the face of dangers at sea.

Today, we have superb sea rescue services which we take very much for granted. The professional Coastguard service keeps watch over our coastline and co-ordinates the rescue services. Most of us will have been impressed by pictures, or perhaps even first-hand sightings, of the life-saving and rescue work by Royal Navy Sea King helicopters and their crews. And, of course, there are the lifeboat services provided by the Royal National Lifeboat Institution. All around the coast, the R.N.L.I. maintains lifeboats whose crews are prepared to go to sea at a moment's notice to rescue those in distress. All are volunteers, committed to helping others, and the whole of the R.N.L.I., in turn, is supported by voluntary contributions from ordinary people.

Personal Qualities

Personal Qualities

If we went back 200 or so years ago, we would find that things were very different. Then the chances of survival for those who were shipwrecked were very small. There was no lifeboat service and certainly none of the other facilities to help in any possible rescue. All that changed, however, in the years after 1838 when a famous rescue took place. The courage and devotion shown by those involved are qualities still seen today in our rescue services.

Grace Darling was a young woman who lived with her elderly father in the lighthouse on Longstone, one of the Farne Islands off the coast of Northumberland in north-east England. Early one September morning in 1838, Grace was woken by cries for help and when she looked out she saw that a ship had been wrecked on the rocks. She woke her father but he was reluctant to launch his boat in the raging storm. However, Grace was sure she could see people moving on the wreck and, determined to help them, she got into the boat. Her father wouldn't let her go by herself, so they rowed off together into the huge seas.

As they got near the wrecked vessel, they could see there were nine people still clinging to it. Grace's father, after several attempts, managed to land on the rock and make his way to the ship. Meanwhile Grace had the dangerous task of rowing off through the wild seas, using all her skill to stop the boat from being dashed to pieces on the rocks. With the help of the shipwrecked crew, the only woman survivor and four men were brought to safety. Two of the men then went back with Grace's father and they managed to bring the others off the wreck. Grace looked after the survivors in the lighthouse for two days until the storm subsided and they could be taken to the mainland.

As a result of her bravery and skill, Grace Darling became a national heroine and her story is still well known. But, perhaps of even greater importance, the event made people realize that, despite the dangers, it was possible to rescue people shipwrecked at sea. It was from this that the idea of setting up a national lifeboat service developed. Today, at lifeboat stations throughout the country, details of the rescues undertaken by lifeboats and their brave crews are proudly recorded.

What was it that gave Grace Darling the strength to show such courage? There are all sorts of possible answers, but many would say that strength of character comes from faith in God and a belief that, whatever the difficulties, there is a purpose in life. It is not always easy to believe this, and many people, young and old alike, experience intense personal difficulties at times, which may threaten to overwhelm them. But, despite such difficulties, everyone does have a purpose in life and a valuable part to play. All of us need the strength of our convictions to believe this and to find our purpose.

This reading is an adaptation of Psalm 23 from the Bible. It uses the metaphor of the sea and suggests that strength to face the troubles of our lives, wherever we live, will come from a faith in God's power.

The Lord is my Pilot; I shall not drift.
He lights me across the dark waters:
He steers me in deep channels.
He keeps my log:
He guides me by the star of holiness
For His name's sake.
Yes, though I sail mid the thunders and tempests of life,
I will dread no danger: for you are near me:
Your love and your care will shelter me.
You prepare a harbour for me in the homeland of eternity;
You anoint the waves with oil, my ship rides calmly.
Surely sunlight and starlight shall favour me on the voyage I take:
And I will rest in the port of my God for ever.

A PRAYER

O God, give us courage – courage to experiment, and not to be afraid of making mistakes; courage to get up when we are down.

Amen.

Personal Qualities

Challenge and Teamwork

* Different sorts of challenges
* Duke of Edinburgh Award Scheme and similar projects
* Personal commitment and determination
* Individual achievement and teamwork: the example of Roger Bannister

If the school has associations with the Duke of Edinburgh Award Scheme or other similar projects, this assembly could be linked with a display or a talk about such organizations. The reading could be read by either a pupil or an adult; it is a long reading and needs to be read well to achieve its dramatic effect. The theme music from the film 'Chariots of Fire' would make a fitting conclusion.

'We are all better than we know; if only we can be brought to realise this, we may never again be prepared to settle for anything less.'

Those are the words of Kurt Hahn, founder of Gordonstoun School and co-founder of the Outward Bound organization. Prince Philip, Duke of Edinburgh, went to Gordonstoun School and was much influenced by Kurt Hahn. The Duke of Edinburgh has a commitment to helping young people and has always believed that they are capable of achieving tremendous things if given the right opportunities. The aim of the Duke of Edinburgh Award Scheme is to provide these opportunities, and the scheme is designed so that anyone of any ability can succeed provided that they have the necessary determination; it is really a matter of each individual doing her or his best.

We all become richer if we set ourselves challenges and try to meet them. The Duke of Edinburgh scheme offers one way of meeting challenges; Outward Bound courses provide another. But there are plenty of others in all aspects of life. For some, challenges are presented through sport; for others, through the mental exercise of the brain; for yet others, they may be through music or the arts, or through a worthwhile hobby; sometimes it may be a combination of these or other activities. The exact nature of the challenge is less important than the commitment, dedication and determination with which it is met.

Very often challenges involve working with others. In such cases teamwork is a vital ingredient of success. Probably the most satisfying challenges are those which require a deep personal commitment within the framework of a team. There is no better illustration of this than Roger Bannister's account of the first time that a mile was run in less than four minutes.

The gun fired. Brasher went into the lead and I slipped in effortlessly behind him, feeling tremendously full of running. My legs seemed to meet no resistance at all, as if propelled by some unknown force.

I barely noticed the half mile, passed in 1 minute 58 seconds, nor when round the next bend, Chataway went into the lead. At three-quarters of a mile the effort was still barely perceptible: the time was 3 minutes 0.7 seconds, and by now the crowd were roaring. Somehow I had to run that last lap in 59 seconds. Chataway led around the next bend and then I pounced past him three hundred yards from the finish.

I had a moment of mixed joy and anguish, when my mind took over. It raced well ahead of my body and drew my body compellingly forward. I felt the moment of a lifetime had come. There was no pain, only a great unity of movement and aim. The world seemed to stand still, or did not exist.

I felt at that moment that it was my one chance to do something supremely well. I drove on, impelled by a combination of fear and pride.

Those last few seconds seemed never-ending. The faint line of the finishing tape stood ahead as a haven of peace, after the struggle. The arms of the world were waiting to receive me if only I reached the tape without slackening my speed. I leapt at the tape like a man taking his last spring to save himself from the chasm that threatens to engulf him.

My effort was over and I collapsed almost unconscious with an arm on either side of me. It was only then that real pain overtook

Personal Qualities

me. I just went on existing in the most passive physical state without being quite unconscious. It was as if all my limbs were caught in an ever-tightening vice. I knew I had done it before I even heard the time.

The stop-watches held the answer. The announcement came – 'Result of one mile ... time 3 minutes' – the rest lost in the roar of excitement. I grabbed Brasher and Chataway, and together we scampered round the track in a burst of spontaneous joy. We had done it – the three of us!

I felt suddenly and gloriously free of the burden of athletic ambition that I had been carrying for years. No words could be invented for such supreme happiness, eclipsing all other feelings. I thought at that moment I could never again reach such a climax of single-mindedness.

(Roger Bannister, *First Four Minutes*)

This is a very moving account of a magnificent achievement that was clearly also a spiritual experience for Roger Bannister. It is unlikely that many of us will face a challenge of that sort in our lives. But, whatever we do, whatever our own challenges are, we will all live a deeper and more satisfying life if we have a determination to succeed and a commitment to work together with other people.

Remember what Kurt Hahn said: 'We are all better than we know; if only we can be brought to realise this, we may never again be prepared to settle for anything less.'

A PRAYER

O God, help us at all times to do the things we ought to do.
Give us:
Clear sight – that we may know what to do;
Courage – to embark on it;
Skill – to find a way through all the problems;
Perseverance – to bring it to its appointed end;
Strength – to resist all the temptations which would lure us aside.

Amen.

Striving to Succeed

❋ The unreal world of cartoons and advertisements
❋ 'Don't give up: try, and try again': the example of Robert the Bruce
❋ Personal rewards of rising to challenges
❋ Turning to God for strength

The hymn 'He who would valiant be' could be sung by those assembled, or by a choir. In smaller group assemblies, a second person could tell the story of Robert the Bruce.

Many young children, and some of us who are not so young, enjoy watching cartoons and animated stories. Most of them are good entertainment. Often the cartoons for young children show lovely places where the world seems ideal and the characters almost too good to be true! Some of you may remember a delightful series of children's programmes several years ago called Camberwick Green and Trumpton. Camberwick Green was a marvellous village where the weather was always fine, where there never seemed to be any school or any problems, and where everyone led a carefree life. Micky Murphy, the baker, always produced perfect loaves; Windy Miller, the miller, helpfully ground the flour as he dodged in and out between the sails. Lord Bellborough's trains always ran to time; when the gentle day's work was done, there was a band concert, and everything was free.

But life is not like this. Things are always going wrong: it's pouring with rain just when you want to go out with a friend; you can't get tickets for the concert you want to go to; tonight's homework is too long and too difficult; you become ill at the beginning of the holidays; worst of all, you have to tidy your bedroom. It's very tempting to try to shape our lives like some ideal cartoon world and advertisements constantly encourage this: use this toothpaste or shampoo, they say, and life will be marvellous; put on this perfume or aftershave and a handsome man or beautiful woman will enter your life. Advertisements for the National Lottery suggest that 'it could be you', reinforcing this unreal view of the world.

But the world is not like this and our lives would be shallow and without meaning if there were no struggles and challenges to face up to. We must respond to them and in doing so our lives will become richer as a result. There is a well-known, true story about Robert the Bruce, King of Scotland about 700 years ago. He was at war with the English, but having been defeated six times he was in a state of despair, not knowing what to do next. After one of these battles he was resting for a while in the hut of a poor fellow countryman. While he sat there wondering what to do, he saw a spider hanging from a long thread, trying to swing itself from one beam to the next in order to fasten its line ready to make a web. It tried many times and failed, but, at last, on the seventh try, it succeeded. Bruce thought, 'That's just like me. I've tried six times and failed. Perhaps, if I try one more time, like the spider, I shall succeed.' And that's what he did; he led his men out into battle, and from then on he was successful.

It's a good story and one that we can learn a lot from. It's saying, 'Don't give up: try again', or, 'If you don't succeed at first, try and try again'. Though we may not be fighting battles like Robert the Bruce, the same philosophy applies to everything in life, from learning to read or swim to succeeding in a job; and, of course, it also applies to our relationships with other people and with the communities around us.

Many people believe that God wants us to become better individuals, and that we are given challenges to help us to do so, but if we take the easy way we won't progress. There are many who, when faced with challenges and difficulties, turn to their God. John Bunyan wrote an inspiring poem in which he demonstrated his trust in his Master – meaning his God. Here is the first verse:

He who would valiant be
'gainst all disaster,
let him in constancy
follow the Master.
There's no discouragement
shall make him once relent,
his first avowed intent
to be a pilgrim.

Camberwick Green and other cartoon places are good fun, but they are not the real world. Let all of us face our difficulties and do our best every day even when it is raining and things are going wrong. Let us remember the story of Robert the Bruce and the spider so that, if at first we don't succeed, we try and try again. If we do these things, we shall find personal reward in our lives, and we shall be able to agree with Bunyan, who ended his famous poem about the journey of the pilgrim through life with these words:

I'll fear not what men say,
I'll labour night and day
to be a pilgrim.

A PRAYER

O God, help us with the hard work and the difficult things we must do. Help us not to give up, but to persevere so that we grow in strength and become better people and help make the world a better place.

Amen.

Being Positive

* Picking out the big things that are right, not the small things that are wrong
* 'Accentuate the positive and eliminate the negative'
* Positive expectations and attitudes

A 'visual aid' of a large sheet of white paper is needed to illustrate a point in this assembly. In the centre of the sheet of paper a small black circle – big enough to be seen at the back of the room – should be drawn. The song could provide an excellent opportunity for a folk group or choir to sing.

Personal Qualities

Personal Qualities

It is sometimes said that there are two ways of looking at life – the positive way or the negative way. We could use two other words – the plus way or the minus way. Here is a simple illustration. What do you see held up in front of you? A small black dot? Does anyone see anything else? Does anyone see a big white rectangle? After all, the white rectangle is far bigger than the black dot.

In our lives at home, at school and in the community, we often pick out and see the small things that are wrong – the minuses – instead of the big things that are right – the pluses. However, our thinking needs to emphasize the pluses, so that we see the good things, then we shall hardly notice the things that are not so good. To use a well-known phrase, we need to 'accentuate the positive and eliminate the negative'.

There is a story of a man who tried to cure himself of negative thinking by giving his wife £1 every time he said a negative thing. He found that he had quite a lot to pay up at the end of the day! She pounced on him if he only said he was afraid it was going to rain. If he feared he wasn't going to sleep very well that night, she demanded instant payment. And if he said he thought he was going to be ill, she wanted double money! Slowly he found the value of the discipline of thinking positively. He expected health. He expected a calm, cheerful day when he woke up. He found a way of life that left no anxious thoughts. The discipline of positive thinking helped to change his whole life.

What qualities do we need to develop so that we emphasize the pluses – the positive features – of life? Some important qualities are to be joyful and loving and to try to create a peaceful atmosphere. A well-known traditional song, often sung as a hymn, speaks of joy, peace and love. These are its words:

Give me joy in my heart, keep me praising,
Give me joy in my heart I pray;
Give me joy in my heart, keep me praising,
Keep me praising till the break of day.

Give me peace in my heart, keep me loving,
Give me peace in my heart I pray,
Give me peace in my heart, keep me loving,
Keep me loving till the break of day.

Give me love in my heart, keep me serving,
Give me love in my heart, I pray,
Give me love in my heart, keep me serving,
Keep me serving till the break of day.

Joy, peace, love – those verses exude happiness and a positive attitude. We need to think of ways – such as these – of being positive, so that it is the pluses of life, rather than the minuses, that are emphasized. To repeat the phrase from earlier on: we need to accentuate the positive and eliminate the negative. Joy in our hearts, peace in our hearts and love in our hearts will go a long way towards bringing happiness into our own lives and into the lives of others with whom we have contact.

A PRAYER

✪

O God, we pray for those whose lives are full of darkness and those for whom the daily pressures of life are great. We ask that they may find ways of enjoying the positive sides of life, and that their burdens may be removed. Help us to appreciate all the good things that are right instead of picking out the small things that are wrong.

Amen.

Personal Qualities

Wisdom, Understanding and Helping Others

* In praise of wisdom, from the Book of Proverbs
* The importance of taking opportunities to acquire wisdom and understanding
* Good neighbourliness as part of everyday life
* The role of the school community in promoting good neighbourliness

There are several opportunities for pupils to participate in this assembly. The reading from Proverbs requires a strong and competent reader, while the second reading could be spoken or sung by a small group (or perhaps using soloists for the verses and the group for the chorus). For the prayer, each line could be spoken by a different person.

Two very different readings link together attitudes to life which can help each of us develop as individuals, and which will also help us contribute successfully to the community. The first reading comes from the Book of Proverbs in the Bible; the writer is offering advice to the listener or reader, and this particular section is in praise of wisdom and understanding. It was written several thousand years ago and needs careful attention to be fully understood. In the language of the time, it is addressing a man, but it is equally relevant to all people – female or male, young or old.

A wise man sees the reason for his father's correction; an arrogant man will not listen to rebuke. A good man enjoys the fruits of righteousness, but violence is meat and drink for the treacherous. He who minds his words preserves his life; he who talks too much comes to grief. A lazy man is torn by appetite unsatisfied, but the diligent grow fat and prosperous. The righteous hate falsehood; the doings of the wicked are foul and deceitful. To do right is the protection of an honest man, but wickedness brings sinners to grief. One man pretends to be rich, although he has nothing; another has great wealth but goes in rags. A rich man must buy himself off, but a poor man is immune from threats. The light of the righteous burns brightly; the embers of the wicked will be put out. A brainless fool causes strife by his presumption; wisdom is found among friends in council. Wealth quickly come by dwindles away, but if it comes little by little, it multiplies. Hope deferred makes the heart sick; a wish come true is a staff of life. To despise a word of advice is to ask for trouble; mind what you are told, and you will be rewarded.

(Proverbs 13:1–13)

That passage is full of advice and wise sayings, but, essentially, it is stressing the importance of acquiring wisdom to gain understanding. And that, surely, is one of the prime reasons for coming to school. School provides opportunities for learning which, in turn, leads to understanding. The acquisition of knowledge and the development of wisdom and understanding are essential elements in the preparation for life, and schools have a vital role to play in this process.

There are other important features of school life that are essential in the preparation for life, and one of these is the necessity to live together in a community. In a school community we are helping one another to develop and grow up; we are learning to live together as good neighbours. Being a good neighbour is a distinguishing feature of a civilized person, so it is a characteristic we should always be striving for.

The second reading is a modern one; it is the words of a song. It is making a plea for us to be good neighbours to everyone in the human race whatever their belief (creed), their colour or their background.

When I needed a neighbour were you there,
Were you there?
When I needed a neighbour were you there?

And the creed and the colour and the name won't matter,
Were you there?

I was hungry and thirsty, were you there,
Were you there? ...

I was cold, I was naked, were you there,
Were you there? ...

Personal Qualities

When I needed a shelter were you there,
Were you there? ...

When I needed a healer were you there,
Were you there? ...

Wherever you travel I'll be there, I'll be there,
Wherever you travel I'll be there.
And the creed and the colour and the name won't matter,
I'll be there.

(Sydney Carter)

The message from those verses is clear: although we are all different, we should all be good neighbours. Most of the time the need for good neighbourliness is not in dramatic or headline-making events – though such instances of neighbourliness are equally important – but in simple, everyday happenings – an act of kindness, a sympathetic word, treating people with courtesy and consideration. All these small things are part of living together as neighbours.

The two readings give us two clear messages to remember, to think about and to act upon, and school provides an excellent environment in which to develop the qualities we will need throughout life. First, we need to use all the opportunities we have to acquire wisdom, because wisdom leads to understanding. Secondly, we need to help each other live together as good neighbours, by thinking and caring about each other.

A PRAYER THAT ASKS GOD TO BE WITH US AS WE TRY OUR BEST IN OUR LIVES

✲

God be in my head, and in my understanding;
God be in my eyes, and in my looking;
God be in my mouth, and in my speaking;
God be in my heart, and in my thinking;
God be at mine end, and in my departing.

Amen.

Ambition and Reward

* Determination to succeed
* Facing challenges: the example of Norman Croucher
* St Paul's challenge to the Corinthians
* Striving for excellence
* Ambition of setting and meeting personal targets

This assembly could be linked with the school's charitable work for disabled people, or could form part of a presentation to a charity supporting disabled people. The two readings can be read by either pupils or adults. Part of Beethoven's Ninth Symphony, or another of his late works, would make an inspiring conclusion, illustrating the composer's triumph over deafness.

There are many fine stories of people's courage in the face of enormous difficulties and of determination to succeed despite overwhelming problems. Such stories can help us in many ways: they can show us what can be achieved through determination, and they can help us to put our own difficulties into perspective. They can also be a source of inspiration in helping us to achieve as much as we can and to reach our full potential. If we are ambitious enough to put our creativity and other talents to work with the earth's abundant and wonderful resources then the world will become a better place.

One inspiring story concerns a man called Norman Croucher, who, at the age of nineteen, was involved in an accident on a railway line and had both legs cut off below the knee by a train. He had been a sportsman and a rock climber before the accident and he was determined that he would not be beaten by this tragedy. Norman mastered his artificial legs as quickly as he could, and, despite the pain, soon started climbing trees and rocks. Before long, he was climbing small mountains. But his ambition was to climb large mountains and in particular he wanted to reach the summit of the Eiger in the Swiss Alps

– surely an impossible task for someone with artificial legs. He needed to build up his strength and decided to do a sponsored walk for Oxfam from John o' Groats to Land's End. He walked from the north-east tip of Scotland to the south-west tip of England in three months, and then he turned his attention to the Eiger. On his third attempt he succeeded in conquering this formidable peak in the Alps, less than five years after his tragic accident. He had faith in himself; he showed what a disabled person could do. From the tragedy of his accident, he achieved something very positive.

Of course we hope that very few, if any, of us will have to cope with a situation as serious as that faced by Norman Croucher while still in his teens. Our challenges may be much more modest, but they are just as real. Very few will come top of the class, or become the best footballer or an outstanding violinist. And, sometimes, simply because we are unlikely to become the best, it is more difficult to motivate ourselves to improve. For example, if you are 4th in a group, it is perhaps easier to improve to become 1st than it is to improve from, say, 25th to 17th; but, in fact, to move up from 25th to 17th may be a far greater achievement than to go from 4th to 1st.

Listen to what St Paul says in a letter to the people of Corinth. He was writing of the difficulties and challenges of being a Christian in a non-Christian country.

> *You know (do you not?) that at the sports all the runners run the race, though only one wins the prize. Like them, run to win! But every athlete goes into strict training. They do it to win a fading wreath; we, a wreath that never fades. For my part, I run with a clear goal before me; I am like a boxer who does not beat the air; I bruise my own body and make it know its master, for fear that after preaching to others I should find myself rejected.*

(1 Corinthians 9:24–27)

Paul was saying that in the challenge you strive for success; you run to win, but when the task is great, you will need to be well prepared, in the same way that athletes go into strict training. You will have to make great efforts, but the rewards for success are immense – your wreath (the prize) will never fade. Drive yourself on, Paul was saying, because your objectives are clear.

Paul's message to the followers in Corinth and the message for us today, surely, is that we should take on challenges. And we must aim to be successful in the challenge. It will undoubtedly take great effort, but success achieved through meeting challenges will bring great satisfaction. Norman Croucher demonstrated that, by striving for excellence despite enormous difficulties, the apparently impossible could be achieved. We can strive for excellence in everything we do; it will require that extra effort and it will demand pride and care in what we do. But the rewards and the sense of satisfaction in a job well done are considerable.

So, be ambitious – not the blind ambition that is the mark of supreme selfishness, but the ambition of setting and meeting challenges and difficulties. Think big, have faith in yourself, seek excellence, and start while you are young! The personal rewards will be immense. One of the most renowned British leaders of the twentieth century, Sir Winston Churchill, gave some good advice to young people. Here is a short extract from his writing.

When I look back on my early years, I cannot but return my sincere thanks to the high gods for the gift of existence. All the days were good and each day better than the other. Ups and downs, risks and journeys, but always the sense of motion, and the illusion of hope. Come on now, all you young people. You are needed more than ever to take your places in life's fighting line. Twenty to twenty-five! These are the years! Don't be content with things as they are. Enter upon your inheritance, accept your responsibilities. Don't take No for an answer. Never submit to failure. You will make mistakes; but as long as you are generous and true, and also fierce, you cannot hurt the world or even seriously distress her. She was made to be wooed and won by youth.

(Winston Churchill, *My Early Life*, slightly adapted)

Personal Qualities

A PRAYER

O God, give us a vision of what must be done, a determination to win through, and courage to overcome all obstacles until we reach the goal.

Amen.

2
Human Behaviour

Doing Things Well

* Temptation to take short cuts
* Satisfaction of doing things well
* Making a thorough start in life
* Advice to a lazy person from the Book of Proverbs

This assembly's theme uses ground elder as an illustration. A piece of this plant – or another with similar characteristics, such as couch grass – could be displayed during the assembly.

Large gardens are very nice; they are places to enjoy, to play in and to relax. However, there is one big snag – there is a lot of work involved in keeping a garden in good condition, and the larger the garden the more work there is. It is very easy for a garden to get overgrown or overrun by weeds. Many people enjoy gardening, but if they don't have enough time they are sometimes tempted to take short-cuts in their gardening work to save time or to get over a particular problem.

One especially nasty weed that can sometimes overwhelm gardens is ground elder or goutweed. It is a plant from the same family as parsley and it has white flowers and creeping underground stems. Its roots spread and spread, and if you want to get rid of it you have to get out

Human Behaviour

every bit of root. If you leave just one centimetre of root, it will start growing again. So getting rid of ground elder is hard, painstaking work and it takes a long time. Gardeners must often wonder whether it's worth it; many times they must be tempted to get the hoe and cut the weed off, and turn over the top few centimetres of soil quickly with a fork. But although this might make the garden look better for a while, in the long term it will be worse because the roots will spread more and more. It's a job that must not be half done: it has to be done thoroughly with care and patience, and by hard work.

This illustration from the garden could be applied to many aspects of life. There is a great deal of truth in the well-known phrase 'If something is worth doing, it's worth doing well'. In our world there is much talk of boredom and unhappiness; we hear too little of satisfaction. But if we do something well, we can get a lot of satisfaction from doing it. If we half do something, frustration and boredom are the likely results. This can apply to school work, to hobbies, to sport, to everything we do.

A gardener can get a feeling of satisfaction in the battle against ground elder and other weeds when the results of the work can be seen. The achievement is considerable, but of course it is only the beginning; there is always work to do in a garden and there will be more to do next year and the year after. However, it is a thorough start and the progress has been real. It is the same with life: if you make a thorough start during your school years, you will make real progress throughout life. But if you are constantly trying to catch up because things were only half done the first time, life will become more difficult and less satisfying. It really is worth doing things thoroughly.

The Book of Proverbs in the Bible contains much useful advice for the reader. One particular section advises a lazy person who does things half-heartedly to take notice of the way of life of an ant. The lazy person – the sluggard – is in danger of ending up in poverty and want.

> *Go to the ant, you sluggard,*
> *watch her ways and get wisdom.*
> *She has no overseer,*
> *no governor or ruler;*
> *but in summer she prepares her store of food*
> *and lays in her supplies at harvest.*

How long, you sluggard, will you lie abed?
When will you rouse yourself from sleep?
A little sleep, a little slumber,
a little folding of the hands in rest,
and poverty will come upon you like a robber,
want like a ruffian.

(Proverbs 6:6–11)

A PRAYER

O God, help us to aim at achievements that are worth pursuing.
Give us single-mindedness, energy and commitment. Whatever
worthy activity we undertake, help us in our efforts never to
settle for second best.

Amen

Fellowship and Friendship

✳ An example of fellowship among senior citizens
✳ Fellowship and friendship in a group of people
✳ Thoughtfulness and companionship
✳ The importance of these qualities in everyday life

The success of this assembly depends on the atmosphere created by a sympathetic reading of the newspaper account. Since the reading is a long one, it might be helpful for someone other than the leader to read it, provided that it is done well.

Listen to this account of a senior citizens' Christmas party taken from the 'Countryside News' section of a local newspaper. The names of the people have been changed.

Human Behaviour

EVERGREEN CHRISTMAS PARTY. For the second consecutive year the committee of the Evergreen Club decided it would be better to have a meal at midday so that the older people could be in their homes again by teatime, for the annual Christmas party, and so the party was preceded by a lunch and not a tea as previously. In the event, with the severe wintry weather it proved to be a wise decision. The tables were attractively decorated with arrangements of evergreens given by Mrs Davies. Mrs Marriot, the catering secretary, organised the meal and was given excellent support by a band of willing and efficient helpers. A hot meal of chicken and chips or fish and chips, according to choice, was brought to the table piping hot by the caterers and was served with bread and pats of butter. The trifles for the dessert were made by committee members. Cheese and biscuits and soft drinks were provided. Sherry was served to the members on arrival at the hall. The President, Mrs L. Johnson, welcomed all present.

After the meal, a grace of thanks was offered by Mr F. Potter, one of the Vice-Presidents. The Secretary, Mrs Doreen Buck, intimated that the committee had decided again to send out parcels of fruit and chocolate with a Christmas card to the older members who are no longer able to attend the meetings, but who were once loyal members of the club. The parcels had been prepared and some distributed by Mr J. Abbott. Mr Abbott had organised a large free draw of 52 beautiful prizes and this draw took place after the meal. The club are most grateful to all donors of these magnificent prizes and thanks and appreciation of their generosity were voiced by the secretary who also thanked Mr Abbott for organising the draw. Mrs Buck also thanked Mrs Marriot and helpers for organising the meal. A Christmas card was received from the Reverend and Mrs M. W. Ashby. The afternoon entertainment was provided by Mrs Susan Sharpe and three of her friends from Littleham and they were accorded a warm welcome by the secretary. A monologue, ' Albert and the Lion', and its sequel, was recited by Mrs Gilbey. Mrs Sarah Higgins, in appropriate costume, sang the old music hall song, 'My Old Man Said Follow the Van', which was followed by a humorous recitation, 'The State I'm In', by Mrs Gilbey. Mrs Morris, an accomplished pianist, played 'The Entertainers', 'Teddy Bears' Picnic', and 'Turkish March' from Beethoven's 'Ruins of Athens'. A short Victorian melodramatic sketch was given by Mrs Biggs and Mrs Gilbey. Old time music hall songs were led by the visitors and heartily sung by the audience and accompanied by Mrs Morris. Mrs Morris also played some light music while cups of tea and mince pies (made by committee members) were handed round. Mrs Johnson thanked the entertainers for coming, especially as the road conditions were so bad. Prior to the arrival of the entertainers, Mr George Meade, a member, accompanied community singing of carols. Mrs Wallis, birthdays secretary, presented gifts to Mrs Joyce Barr, Mrs Sandra Kiddy, Mrs Emma Martin, Mrs Doreen Wilson and Mr Reg Frost. Members were reminded that the next meeting would be on January 9th. Those who gave prizes for the draw were: (a list of all fifty-two donors of prizes and their gifts is included.)

That account describes a world very different from the day-to-day lives of most of us, but, despite that, there are some underlying themes in that passage which should be as important to us as they are to the elderly people in that village in the heart of the countryside where the Evergreen Club meets. (Pause for a few seconds to allow reflection on the themes.) The themes that come across in that article are: love, compassion and, above all, fellowship and friendship. Let's analyse the article in a bit more detail.

First, the writer. What kind of person wrote that article? A man or a woman? We don't know and it doesn't matter, but we'll assume the writer is a woman. We can form an image of her – a kind person who would do anything to help someone else, immensely loyal, and a person who can always be relied on. She would never miss a deadline to get her story to the Editor! Think of the care she has put into the article: everyone is mentioned – no one must be missed out; all those with birthdays are named, all fifty-two donors of prizes – everyone. But the article is more than a list; she has taken much trouble to think of different phrases and ways of saying things. In reporting the facts, the writer goes out of her way to be complimentary: 'with the severe wintry weather, it proved to be a wise decision', 'excellent band of willing and efficient helpers', 'the older members who are no longer able to attend the meetings, but were once loyal members of the club', and so on. So the writer comes over as a friendly, kind person with a deeply sympathetic view of human nature.

Human Behaviour

What of the Evergreen Club itself? It is a group where lots of people work together for the enjoyment of others and themselves. So many people were involved – the table decorators, the cooks, the servers, the entertainers, the draw organizers. The thoughtfulness and companionship of the Club is most noticeable – for example, remembering those who could not come and those who had birthdays, the profuse thanks given to all who helped. The whole atmosphere at the Club must have been delightful, whether it was during the meal, during the hearty singing of carols, or in the laughter following the story of 'Albert and the Lion' which, no doubt, most people had heard at least fifty times before.

This Evergreen Club of Senior Citizens is, indeed, very different from the world of most of us here, but, although the circumstances may be different, the truths demonstrated in the article are universal. So the next time any of us are tempted to be inconsiderate or unkind, or to ignore the friend who needs help, let us remember the warmth and friendship and support generated within the Evergreen Club, and try to make our own lives as positive and caring as theirs.

A PRAYER

✪

O God, in every friendship we have, help us to put our friends before ourselves. May we never selfishly make use of our friends purely for our own pleasure or purposes, but try to help them and all whom we know in a positive and constructive way.

Amen.

Giving and Our Conscience

❋ The development and work of the Salvation Army
❋ Material wealth and spiritual wealth
❋ Looking at our own conscience
❋ Individual action and the action of governments
❋ Sincerity in giving and helping

This assembly provides an opportunity to invite members of the local branch of the Salvation Army to attend. You could also arrange for the school band or choir to play or sing a hymn such as 'Onward Christian Soldiers'. The extracts from the War Cry could be read by two different pupils or adults.

In the nineteenth century the conditions of life for thousands of poor people in London and other large cities in Britain were appalling. The contrast between the deprivation of their lives and the comfortable lifestyles of many others was enormous. However, there were a number of people who devoted much of their lives to helping those who had no alternative to living in poverty. Notable among such people were members of an organization called the Salvation Army.

Founded in 1865 by William Booth, the Salvation Army was a Christian body dedicated to social work amongst the poor. Its work still continues today. Its members show their Christian faith in the most public of ways – by wearing a distinctive uniform. In its outreach work, the Salvation Army is prepared to get involved in areas which many people would prefer to ignore or forget. Its work with destitute people, its hostels for the homeless, its passionate caring for the have-nots – these thing and many more are proof of the sincerity and faith of members of the Salvation Army.

The organization produces a newspaper called the *War Cry*. Its members often go into pubs and other public places at weekends, with collecting boxes and selling copies of the *War Cry*. The paper describes some of the work of the Salvation Army and also tries to offer helpful advice on problems facing individuals and the world generally.

Human Behaviour

Sometimes it has a 'Problems Page' featuring letters from readers and replies by an expert. Many issues are discussed on this page and the example we are going to hear addresses a moral problem that many people face. A reader wrote the following letter:

I am troubled that while half the world is starving we are watching our colour televisions, driving our cars and enjoying every comfort (and even complaining about our lot as well). The alternative – to give away everything – seems extreme. Is there a proper balance that can be reached?

This was the reply that was given, slightly adapted here:

You have highlighted a dilemma with which many will identify. When we compare our lot with others – the haves with the have-nots – it is proper that we should pause and take stock.

In every day and age, a few take quite literally Jesus' words to the rich young ruler (to give all his wealth to the poor). It is clear, however, from the context of the story, that the reason for this advice being given was not the plight of the needy but because the man's wealth was the cause of his own inner poverty.

In any case, however wealthy he might have been, it would have been only a drop in the ocean in relation to the size of the problem. And, as far as the individual is concerned, this is still the case. If all readers of this column gave to a particular charity every penny they possess it would be a reasonable sum of money, but how far would it go? And what about other equally deserving charities?

It is encouraging that any disaster, even in a far-distant land, will call forth a remarkable response. That is, if it hits our television screens! But what about the vaster problem of the starving millions? It is obvious that as far as the developing parts of the world are concerned, help must come from the more wealthy nations. Part of our moral duty is to encourage our own government to increase – rather than decrease – our national contribution to the Third World.

But what of our personal giving? It is a case of establishing priorities, for no one can give to every worthy cause. Everyone must find their own level of giving in relation to their income and their own legitimate needs and responsibilities. A proper balance can be achieved, but it has to be sought by each individual. And in this regard everyone needs an almighty sincerity, and a willingness sometimes to say no to oneself.

Finally, we must always beware of imagining that the solution we have found should be generally accepted. The important thing is to educate our own conscience, and then let our generosity be unostentatious.

The question and the response focus our minds on a number of points. First, the need to distinguish between material wealth and spiritual wealth, and between material poverty and spiritual poverty. (By spiritual wealth and poverty is meant the richness or otherwise of our own inner lives – not the material things we possess, but our mental and emotional resources.) Material wealth may possibly be the cause of spiritual wealth, but that is not necessarily so; equally, material poverty may be the cause of spiritual poverty, but the one certainly does not necessarily lead to the other.

Secondly, the need to distinguish between the actions of governments and of individuals, but also the need to recognize the importance of both. What an individual gives or does may not in itself be much, but the responsibility of each person to himself or herself is very important.

Thirdly, the need to look at our own consciences so that we can try to work out in our own minds how we should act. This should not lead to an 'I'm better than you' attitude, or an attitude that says, 'I've given away £100 to charity this year, so aren't I good?'. But, as the article says, we need to find 'an almighty sincerity, and a willingness sometimes to say no to oneself'.

Finally, the last sentence of the article is worth thinking about again: 'The important thing is to educate our own conscience, and then let our generosity be unostentatious.'

A PRAYER

O God, give us an honest mind, a responsive heart, and a generous hand.

Amen.

Human Behaviour

Human Behaviour

Hypocrisy

* The meaning of hypocrisy
* The breakdown of trust and respect
* Being honest with others
* Jesus' views on judging others

There are several opportunities here for involving pupils in the assembly. In particular, the first two extracts lend themselves to dramatization by two people – one person reading out the letter, the other miming the reactions of the recipient. The two extracts from St Matthew could be read by two other pupils or adults.

This is a letter I received recently. (You could either read the two extracts below or use a similar example of 'junk' mail that you have received yourself.)

```
Dear Mr/Ms ... (name),
There could be an attractive MYSTERY GIFT waiting at
this moment to be sent to you at ... (address). To
find out if there is, just look inside the small red
envelope enclosed.
    And there's the chance of riches too! You have
been selected unanimously by our Customer Awards
Committee to receive no fewer than SIX numbers in our
£250,000 'LUCKY BREAK' PRIZE DRAW, and any one of them
could already have won you a prize - maybe the first
prize of £100,000!
    Just think what a marvellous feeling it would be
to stroll into your bank with a cheque for £100,000 to
pay into your account. And, Mr/Ms ... (name), you
could have two bites at this succulent cherry!
    If the holder of the winning number fails to
return it to us, our computer will automatically
```

reallocate that prize to whoever returns the next nearest number – and that could be you!

By the same token, any prize that you failed to claim could go to someone else – so make sure you send back your numbers promptly! If you return them within 14 days, you'll also stand a chance of collecting a £10,000 bonus.

Most people receive letters like this from time to time, perhaps accompanied by important-sounding documents like the following:

CERTIFICATE OF CUSTOMER APPRECIATION

This is to certify that ... (name) is a loyal and valued customer and as such is entitled to receive

A Special Customer Appreciation Award

This award is non-transferable and is presented in recognition of the above-named person's outstanding record of custom with our company.

Signed ...

CUSTOMER SERVICES MANAGER
CONTEST MANAGER

This sort of mail is becoming increasingly common. This particular one was, in fact, part of an attempt to persuade those receiving it to buy a book on gardening.

As well as being an example of dreadful, gushing writing, the extract brings out some of the worst features of advertising. Its chief fault is that it is hypocritical. ('Hypocritical' means pretending to be what you are not.) So what is hypocritical in this letter?

First, it is pretending to be a personal letter to me: my own name is mentioned several times, and my address once. It seems that someone has taken the care to write a personal letter. That is nonsense: the computer has been programmed to put in the right words at the right places. Secondly, it implies that I'm incredibly lucky to take part in the draw: 'you have been selected unanimously by our Customer Awards Committee'. In fact, probably hundreds of thousands of people have had an identical letter. Thirdly, it tries to excite the reader by the contents of the Red Envelope. Have I been awarded a mystery gift? Of course I have! It would not have been sent if I hadn't. Finally, there is the suggestion that the gift has been carefully chosen for me. But no doubt it is the same gift for everyone – women or men, young or old – not really much of a personal gift!

Of course, most people will probably see through this example of hypocrisy. So what's wrong with hypocrisy? Increasingly, it leads to the breakdown of trust and respect. And without trust and respect, life in our complex society becomes even more difficult. People become cynical, which is a negative, distrustful outlook on life.

People are cynical about hypocritical politicians who promise that they can solve problems and difficulties when they know that they can't. The person who dresses in her best clothes to go to church to show how good she is, and then ignores pleas to help starving people, is a hypocrite. The pop star who sings protest songs about inequality in this country, and then becomes a tax exile in Jersey, is a hypocrite.

Are you a hypocrite? Think about the sort of people you trust and respect. Is it because they don't pretend to be something they are not? We should not pretend to be virtuous when we know we are not, but we should try to be honest with everyone. Jesus had some excellent words of advice on this subject, as these two readings from St Matthew's Gospel illustrate.

Alas for you, lawyers and Pharisees, hypocrites! You clean the outside of cup and dish, which you have filled inside by robbery and self-indulgence! Blind Pharisee! Clean the inside of the cup first; then the outside will be clean also. Alas for you, lawyers and Pharisees, hypocrites! You are like tombs covered with whitewash; they look well from the outside, but inside they are full of dead men's bones and all kinds of filth. So it is with you: outside you look like honest men, but inside you are brim-full of hypocrisy and crime.

(Matthew 23:25–27)

Pass no judgement, and you will not be judged. For as you judge others, so you will yourselves be judged, and whatever measure you deal out to others will be dealt out to you. Why do you look at the speck of sawdust in your brother's eye, with never a thought for the great plank in your own? Or how can you say to your brother, 'Let me take the speck out of your eye', when all the time there is the plank in your own? You hypocrite! First take the plank out of your own eye, and then you will see clearly to take the speck out of your brother's ... Ask, and you will receive; seek, and you will find; knock, and the door will be opened. For everyone who asks receives, he who seeks finds, and to him who knocks, the door will be opened ... Always treat others as you would like them to treat you.

(Matthew 7:1–12)

'Clean the inside of the cup first; then the outside will be clean also.' That is excellent advice, and essential if we are to live in a civilized society. If we do this, we shall not be guilty of hypocrisy.

A PRAYER

O God, give us the strength and the wisdom to be honest and not to pretend that we are better than we are. With your help and with the help of others, we will endeavour to make our contribution to a civilized society in which we treat others as we would wish to be treated by them.

Amen.

Human Behaviour

Judging Others

* Discerning the truth
* Making judgements about others
* Recognizing our own faults

This assembly follows on from the assembly on hypocrisy by using one of the same readings and developing similar ideas. The two assemblies could be used on consecutive occasions. Alternatively, this one might be used with younger or less sophisticated pupils. A visual aid of a toy elephant or giraffe or other animal, concealed in a pocket until the vital moment, is essential! The reading from St Matthew could be read by a pupil or an adult.

We're going to begin this assembly by listening to a reading that we have used before:

(The reading from Matthew 7:1–12 on page 47 should be read.)

How do you decide whether you like someone? How do you decide whether someone is telling the truth? Sometimes it is easy to know whether something is right or wrong. If you say that someone is wearing spectacles or has black hair, it is straightforward for anyone to tell whether or not you are right. Sometimes it is not so easy. If someone said the following things, how would you decide if they were telling the truth?

I have a handkerchief in my pocket.
I have £1000 in my pocket.
I have an elephant/giraffe in my pocket.

With regard to the handkerchief, the person is probably telling the truth. After all, handkerchiefs do go into pockets and most people usually have at least one handkerchief in a pocket. However, on

occasions, you might forget to put one in, or, for some other reason, you might not have one. But if someone says they have a handkerchief in their pocket, you will probably believe them.

But what about the person who says they have £1000 in their pocket? This is less likely to be true because not many people carry £1000 in their pocket. Even if you were lucky enough to have £1000, it would be rather foolish to carry it around in a pocket. But you can't be sure that the person is lying, because money is often carried in pockets and it would be possible to get £1000 into a pocket, especially if it was all in £50 notes. Nonetheless, it is unlikely that they are telling the truth. As for the person who claims to have an elephant in their pocket, that's quite ridiculous because elephants don't go into pockets. Clearly the person is not telling the truth. The first two examples, however, show that it is not always easy to come to a judgement without having all the necessary information available.

Sometimes people change their views of others when circumstances change. A story about changing circumstances is the basis of a well-known play by J. B. Priestley, called *When we are married*. In the play, three couples, who had all got married on the same day, had fairly definite opinions of each other. But then it was discovered that the young minister had not been properly authorized to carry out weddings, so they were not actually married. At first they were all shocked, but then they began to view each other very differently. Annie Parker felt able to stand up for herself and say to her husband what she had long thought – that he was very dull, very, very dreary, and stingy. And Herbert Soppitt now summoned up the courage to tell his wife what he really thought of her but had been afraid to do so. The play is a comedy and has a happy ending, but it makes people think about how we judge others in real life.

Why do you look at the speck of sawdust in your brother's eye, with never a thought for the great plank in your own?... First take the plank out of your own eye, and then you will see clearly to take the speck out of your brother's.

Jesus is saying, 'Don't criticize someone for a tiny fault (the speck of dust), when you have a lot of faults of your own (the plank)'. The reading ends with the advice, 'Always treat others as you would like them to treat you'. You see, after all, you might be wrong in your

Human Behaviour

judgement. (Produce the toy elephant from your pocket.) In fact, I have got an elephant in my pocket!

A PRAYER

O God, help us to care about other people, whether we like them or not. The unpopular, the handicapped and the weak need our special concern. Help us to be generous in the way we treat other people, just as we should like to be treated generously by them.

Amen.

Good and Evil

❋ The presence of good and evil in all of us
❋ Choosing between right and wrong
❋ Evil triumphs when good people do nothing
❋ Stand up and be counted in the fight against evil

We sometimes hear reports, on television or in the newspapers, of incidents of cruelty or violence that horrify all decent people. It seems scarcely possible that such things could happen and they force us to ask ourselves questions about the nature of our society and what response we should make to such events.

After the conviction of two boys for the murder of a small toddler, the judge said, 'It was an act of unparalleled evil and barbarity.' What is meant by 'evil'? What is meant by 'good'? Why, in this particular case, did two ordinary boys commit such a crime?

Many other questions spring to mind, particularly questions relating to good and evil. Most religions and moral codes state that there is such a thing as absolute evil and absolute good, and that we need to distinguish between the two. In addition, most people take the view that in every human being there is an inclination to the good and an inclination to the evil. Both are there, and either can become dominant. The point of a moral life is to make a choice and to choose the good. The two boys referred to earlier chose the evil. Why? Why do some people choose the evil? Will you always choose the good?

A famous politician once said that all that is needed for evil to triumph is for good people to do nothing. We saw that in the horrors of the concentration camps in Nazi Germany. We see it too often today in areas of conflict and violence in the world, and, on a smaller scale, we see it around us in school and elsewhere when things happen that are wrong and no one does anything about it. We pretend we haven't noticed or we turn the other way. This short reading is called 'When to speak'.

> *In Germany, the Nazis came for the Communists and I didn't speak up because I was not a Communist. Then they came for the Jews and I didn't speak up because I wasn't a Jew. Then they came for the Trade Unionists and I didn't speak up because I was not a Trade Unionist. Then they came for the Catholics and I was a Protestant so I didn't speak up. Then they came for me ...*
> *By that time there was no-one to speak up for anyone.*

(Martin Niemöller)

We all need to recognize that everyone is capable of both good and evil, and that we must control and contain the potential for evil. What is right and what is wrong must be made very clear, both within the school community and in society as a whole. Bullying is an evil and will not be accepted; sexual harassment and indecent assault are evil and will not be tolerated. Although we all have within us the capacity for both good and evil, most people are fundamentally good and know what is right and what is wrong. We must always choose the good.

But we must also remember the quotation mentioned earlier – that all that is needed for evil to triumph is for good people to do nothing – and the reading which illustrates that point. We must never let that happen – either at home, at school, in the streets, at work or at play. Whatever the circumstances, we must never let it happen anywhere. All good people – and that means all of us – must stand up and be

Human Behaviour

counted. We must not turn away and let evil triumph. We must ensure that we speak, not of the triumph of evil, but of the triumph of good.

A PRAYER

O God, the source of all goodness, we ask for your blessing on all of us so that we are able to distinguish between good and evil, and always choose the good.

Amen.

St Valentine's Day and Love

✳ Different sorts of love
✳ Love as an essential part of human experience
✳ Sharing – giving and taking
✳ Care and concern for others

As an introduction to this assembly recordings of one or two songs about love could be played; they might be pop songs, folk songs or extracts from operatic arias.

February 14th, as everyone knows, is St Valentine's Day – a day for love, a day to show care and concern for loved ones. Indeed caring and loving complement each other; you cannot have one without the other. Love has become an overused word, and somewhat devalued, which is a shame because, in its fullest sense, love is the supreme human emotion and the most wonderful to experience. This sort of love is quite different from the superficial pleasure experienced, for instance, by someone who says, 'I love ice cream', or the delight felt by people who say they love the music of a particular composer or pop group. There is also a great difference between the intensely personal love between two people and the deep affection that many people have for friends, relatives or organizations and community groups to which they are committed.

The ways in which love is expressed are equally varied and may change over time. For example, the love between two people may be more passionate and openly expressed in the earlier stages, but the intensity of the love can develop in different ways throughout the lives of the couple. All love, in its many and varied ways, is equally valid. The songwriter who wrote that love makes the world go round knew something of the importance of love. Some of the greatest literature is about love, and it is a constant topic in music of all types. So much has been written on the subject of love that it is very difficult to select just one example to do justice to it. This short extract from a book by the Russian writer Leo Tolstoy demonstrates that love is an essential part of human experience.

> *People think there are circumstances when one may deal with human beings without love, but no such circumstances ever exist. Inanimate objects may be dealt with without love: we may fell trees, bake bricks, hammer iron without love. But human beings cannot be handled without love, any more than bees cannot be handled without care. That is the nature of bees. If you handle bees carelessly you will harm the bees and yourself as well. And so it is with people. And it cannot be otherwise, because mutual love is the fundamental law of human life.*

(L. N. Tolstoy, *Resurrection*)

What, then, is love all about? As we have already indicated, it is about all sorts of things, not least of which is sharing – about giving as well as taking. Learning to live with others is very important. One day, probably, you will choose the person with whom you wish to set up home. Then, if your home is to be happy, there will have to be plenty of sharing, plenty of giving as well as taking. You may have already thought of the sort of person you would like to live with: perhaps you have sent that person a Valentine card! As we have said already, caring and loving are really parts of the same thing. We can all practise being

Human Behaviour

kind and considerate, at home, at school and in the community. In this way we demonstrate that we care for and love others – not necessarily in a romantic way, but in just as deep and sincere a way.

But what has St Valentine to do with lovers? The answer is nothing at all! Like so many obscure saints, very little is known about him. It just happened that the day dedicated to him in the Church's calendar, February 14th, fell at the time when it was believed that birds began to mate and young people might be looking for partners to marry. So, for hundreds of years, St Valentine's Day has been a celebration of love. We should use it as an opportunity to show our love for those who are dear to us, and our concern for others in a true and caring way.

A PRAYER

O God, we ask you to bless those whom we love, those who are dear to us, and those whom we care about. Bless our families and our friends, and help us to live in such a way that we may never be untrue, unfaithful or disloyal to them.

Amen.

True Friends

* Fair-weather friends – the example of Piglet
* Standing by friends
* Temptation to 'jump on the bandwagon'

The extract from Winnie-the-Pooh could be acted out, with four people taking the parts of the Narrator, Winnie-the-Pooh, Piglet and Christopher Robin. The leader might wish to be the narrator, but this is not essential. The extract could be shortened if necessary, although read with expression and humour, it is usually greatly enjoyed by older students.

One of the delights of having young children in the house is being able to read children's books! Many children's books can be read at different levels: as well as providing a good story which young children can enjoy, there is much that older children and adults may find thought-provoking. Lots of young children are very fond of the stories by A. A. Milne about Winnie-the-Pooh, Christopher Robin, Piglet and others. The stories are great fun, but behind them are some interesting thoughts about people's characters. Listen to an extract from one of these stories. Winnie-the-Pooh is described by Christopher Robin as a 'silly old Bear', but it is interesting to see the character of Piglet in this story.

One fine winter's day when Piglet was brushing away the snow in front of his house, he happened to look up, and there was Winnie-the-Pooh. Pooh was walking round and round in a circle, thinking of something else, and when Piglet called to him, he just went on walking.

'Hello!' said Piglet, 'What are you doing?'

'Hunting,' said Pooh.

'Hunting what?'

'Tracking something,' said Winnie-the-Pooh very mysteriously.

'Tracking what?' said Piglet, coming closer.

'That's just what I ask myself. I ask myself, What?'

'What do you think you'll answer?'

'I shall have to wait until I catch up with it,' said Winnie-the-Pooh. 'Now, look there.' He pointed to the ground in front of him. 'What do you see there?'

'Tracks,' said Piglet. 'Paw marks.' He gave a little squeak of excitement. 'Oh, Pooh! Do you think it's a-a-a Woozle?'

'It may be,' said Pooh. 'Sometimes it is, and sometimes it isn't. You never can tell with paw marks.'

With these few words he went on tracking, and Piglet, after watching him for a minute or two, ran after him. Winnie-the-Pooh had come to a sudden stop, and was bending over the tracks in a puzzled sort of way.

'What's the matter?' asked Piglet.

'It's a very funny thing,' said Bear, 'but there seem to be two animals now. This – whatever-it-was – has been joined by another –

Human Behaviour

Human Behaviour

whatever-it-is – and the two of them are now proceeding in company. Would you mind coming with me, Piglet, in case they turn out to be Hostile Animals?'

Piglet scratched his ear in a nice sort of way, and said that he had nothing to do until Friday, and would be delighted to come, in case it really was a Woozle.... So off they went together.

There was a small spinney of larch-trees just here, and it seemed as if the two Woozles, if that was what they were, had been going round this spinney; so round this spinney went Pooh and Piglet after them.... And still the tracks went on in front of them.

Suddenly Winnie-the-Pooh stopped, and pointed excitedly in front of him. 'Look!'

'What?' said Piglet, with a jump. And then, to show that he hadn't been frightened, he jumped up and down once or twice more in an exercising sort of way.

'The tracks!' said Pooh. 'A third animal has joined the other two!'

'Pooh!' cried Piglet. 'Do you think it is another Woozle?'

'No' said Pooh, 'because it makes different marks. It is either Two Woozles and one, as it might be, Wizzle, or Two, as it might be, Wizzles and one, if so it is, Woozle. Let us continue to follow them.'

So off they went, feeling just a little anxious now, in case the three animals in front of them were of Hostile Intent.... And then, all of a sudden, Winnie-the-Pooh stopped again, and licked the tip of his nose in a cooling manner, for he was feeling more hot and anxious than ever in his life before. There were four animals in front of them!

'Do you see, Piglet? Look at their tracks! Three, as it were, Woozles, and one, as it was, Wizzle. Another Woozle has joined them!'

And so it seemed to be. There were the tracks; crossing over each other here, getting muddled up with each other there; but, quite plainly every now and then, the tracks of four sets of paws.

'I think,' said Piglet, when he had licked the tip of his nose, and found that it brought very little comfort, 'I think that I have just remembered something that I forgot to do yesterday and shan't be able to do to-morrow. So I suppose I really ought to go back and do it now.'

'We'll do it this afternoon, and I'll come with you,' said Pooh.

'It isn't the sort of thing you can do in the afternoon,' said Piglet *quickly. 'It's a very particular morning thing, that has to be done in the morning, and, if possible, between the hours of - What would you say the time was?'*

'About twelve,' said Winnie-the-Pooh, looking at the sun.

'Between, as I was saying, the hours of twelve and twelve five. So, really, dear old Pooh, if you'll excuse me - What's that?'

Pooh looked up at the sky, and then, as he heard the whistle again, he looked up at the branches of a big oak tree, and then he saw a friend of his.

'It's Christopher Robin,' he said.

'Ah, then you'll be all right,' said Piglet. 'You'll be quite safe with him. Good-bye,' and he trotted off home as quickly as he could, very glad to be Out of All Danger again.

Christopher Robin came slowly down the tree.

'Silly old Bear,' he said, 'what were you doing? First you went round the spinney twice by yourself, and then Piglet ran after you and you went round again together, and then you were just going round a fourth time -'

'Wait a minute,' said Winnie-the-Pooh, holding up his paw.

He sat down and thought, in the most thoughtful way he could think. Then he fitted his paw into one of the Tracks ... and then he scratched his nose twice, and stood up.

'Yes,' said Winnie-the-Pooh.

'I see now,' said Winnie-the-Pooh.

'I have been Foolish and Deluded,' said he, 'and I am a Bear of No Brain at All.'

'You're the Best Bear in All the World,' said Christopher Robin soothingly.

What sort of person is Piglet? Is he the sort of person you could trust? Would he make a real friend? Has he got strength of character? In this story Piglet's character is not a particularly attractive one. At first he's very excited. It'll be great fun helping Pooh to go Woozle hunting; after all, he's a bit bored and he's got nothing to do until Friday. But he soon begins to get frightened, although he doesn't want to show it. Then, of course, he suddenly remembers his important appointment between 'twelve and twelve five', and disappears very quickly. Does he support his friend in time of trouble? No! He is keen

Human Behaviour

to join in when it seems to be fun, but he is equally keen to drop out when things become difficult.

This weakness in character is something we need to guard against if we are to provide the right sort of support for our friends. Sometimes it occurs the other way round, when people join in because they haven't the strength to say 'no'. The phrase 'jumping on the bandwagon' may be used to describe the actions of someone who joins in because he or she thinks it is the fashionable thing to do, or the popular thing to do, or that they would be favoured by doing so. Following the leader, doing what the gang is doing because it's the easy thing to do, doing what you think will please others rather than what you think is right – these are the temptations, but are they always right? Have you got the strength of character to resist if you know that something is wrong?

Watch out for false friends who are only around when things are going well, like Piglet in our story. Equally, make sure that you are not false to your friends, or to anyone who needs your support. Actions usually speak louder than words, and you will be judged by what you do.

A PRAYER

O God, help us to support our friends whenever they need us and help us always to do what is right. Give us the wisdom to distinguish right from wrong, and the strength to resist the temptation to follow the crowd into actions that will bring harm.

Amen.

Opportunities and Temptations

* Comparing life with the game of Snakes and Ladders
* Opportunities for progress – ladders
* Temptations that drag us down – snakes
* Making the right choices
* The temptation of Jesus in the wilderness

Most people are familiar with the game of Snakes and Ladders, and many of us will have played it at some time. Let's imagine the Snakes and Ladders board and, with a little imagination, see it as representing the development of our lives.

We can think of the ladders as the opportunities that we are presented with; the snakes are temptations that try to drag us down as we journey through life. Snakes are twisting, turning, devious; they curve into 'S' shapes - S for selfishness, sin, and, in the Bible story we shall hear, for Satan. Ladders are straight and direct; they lead forwards and upwards. In the ladder, you can see the letter 'L' – L for loyalty and love.

Notice something else about the board. The ladders start at different places: some are on the bottom line at the beginning of life's journey, while others present opportunities at various stages along the way. But there are also snakes everywhere, even on the top line. No part of the journey of life is easy: there are temptations trying to drag us down at every stage.

But there is a fundamental difference between the game of Snakes and Ladders and the journey of life. In the game it is chance that lands us on the snakes or the ladders; in life it is a matter of choice – to take the opportunities and go forward, or to be tempted and dragged down. We ought always to be striving for our ideals, for perfection – straight up the ladders, which perhaps lead to our idea of God. But then there is Satan trying to tempt us, trying to drag us down. Which choice will you make?

When you have important decisions to make, it is sometimes

Human Behaviour

helpful to be by yourself so that you can think things out quietly without being disturbed. The right decision is not always the easy one or the most popular one. In the period called Lent, the Christian Church remembers the time when Jesus wanted to be alone with God so that he could discover the right way to bring people to God, rather than being tempted to choose the easy way by doing things that would be spectacular or instantly popular. Other religions have similar periods of reflection when people are encouraged to think of the things that are really important so that the trivial and the worthless are put to one side.

The story of the temptation of Jesus is told in the Gospel of St Matthew:

Then Jesus was led by the Spirit into the desert to be tempted by the devil. After fasting for forty days and forty nights, he was hungry. The tempter came to him and said, 'If you are the Son of God, tell these stones to become bread.' Jesus answered, 'It is written: "Man does not live by bread alone, but on every word that comes from the mouth of God."'

Then the devil took him to the holy city and had him stand on the highest point of the temple. 'If you are the Son of God,' he said, 'throw yourself down. For it is written: "He will command his angels concerning you, and they will lift you up in their hands, so that you will not strike your foot against a stone."' Jesus answered him, 'It is also written: "Do not put the Lord your God to the test."' Again, the devil took him to a very high mountain and showed him all the kingdoms of the world and their splendour. 'All this I will give you,' he said , 'If you will bow down and worship me.' Jesus said to him, 'Away from me, Satan! For it is written: "Worship the Lord your God, and serve him only."' Then the devil left him.

(Matthew 4:1–10)

•••

A PRAYER

O God, in all the hazards of life, give us courage that comes not from physical power but from what we believe to be right. In times of temptation, danger and difficulty, let us not take the easy way out, but give us strength to act in the best interests of all people.

Amen.

Human Behaviour

3

Learning from Experience

Learning to Drive

* Learning tolerance of and dependence on others
* Learning humility: acknowledging mistakes
* Learning from experiences
* Recognizing that learning is part of life

With some adaptations, this assembly would lend itself to role-play. As an introduction to the theme, an adult and an older pupil could act out a short scene of a parent teaching a daughter or son to drive.

There are many significant dates in young people's lives. For many, one of the most important is their seventeenth birthday, for that marks the date when they can first drive a car on public roads. But, who is going to teach them to drive, and who is going to be with them as they practise?

Sometimes parents are able to help; sometimes lessons from a professional driving instructor are the answer. In many cases, it is a combination of the two. If a parent is willing and able to teach their daughter or son to drive, it can be a testing time for relationships. In fact, many parents refuse to teach their offspring to drive because it is too disruptive an experience for driver and instructor alike. They are too close to each other. It can be just as difficult for a husband or wife to teach each other to drive.

However, if a parent and a daughter or son are able to manage the process, they usually find that they both learn a lot not only about driving but about each other. The parent learns to reassess driving techniques, thinking consciously about things that have been done by instinct for perhaps twenty years or more. They will realize that experience alone is not enough to teach someone else. You've got to be clear in your mind about what needs to be explained. For example, how exactly do you use the clutch, or what do you do with your hands when you turn round a sharp bend? You also have to get the right balance between encouragement and criticism. Too much encouragement will induce a false sense of security; too much criticism will demoralize the learner. The skills of any good teacher are brought into frequent use!

The daughter or son learns a lot as well. They may even discover that a parent is not too bad after all! Instead of being someone who is a bit of a nuisance but has to be tolerated, they can be quite useful. Without the parent, the daughter or son cannot drive the car. Young people have been known to enquire very considerately about weekend and evening appointments! They might even volunteer to help on shopping trips, and suggest additional visits to grandparents. In other words, they learn a lot about tolerance and dependence on others.

They may also learn much about humility. Most young people make excellent progress, but even so they find learning to drive harder than they thought it would be. Most think that driving will be easy – after all, most adults manage to do it more or less successfully, so there should be no problem. However, most soon realize that driving a car is a complex and skilful operation requiring care, concentration and the ability to carry out a number of complicated processes at the same time. Inevitably, they will make mistakes and things will go wrong. When that happens the best thing to do is to acknowledge what has gone wrong because that is the way to make progress. If, say, after stalling the car for the third time when attempting to pull away from a set of traffic lights, the learner is able to say, 'I made a mess of that, didn't I?', then, indeed, that person will learn from his or her mistake. The recognition that you have a lot to learn is the essence of humility.

The process of learning to drive is in some ways a reflection of life as a whole. If we believe that we know it all, that we don't need other people, that we are better than others in some way, then we won't

Learning from Experience

realize how little we really know and how much we have to learn from others. Similarly, if we are not prepared to help others and use our skills and experiences in a constructive, sympathetic and sensitive way, then we are being selfish and not contributing to society. If, however, we believe that we can always learn something as we add to our own experiences of life, if we believe that working with others is more productive than working against others, and if we are able to acknowledge our weaknesses, then our lives will be fuller. We shall also enrich the lives of those around us.

A PRAYER

O God, we acknowledge that we are often quick to condemn those with whom we disagree. Help us to value other people and what they say and do, and give us the humility to recognize our own weaknesses.

Amen.

Friendship and the Journey through Life

✳ Building on experiences
✳ The importance of friendship
✳ Valuing our friends
✳ Aesop's fable about false friends

There's a story about a traveller who had lost his way and stopped to ask a local person how to get to a certain place. The local scratched his head and thought for a while, and then said, 'Well, if I was going there, I wouldn't start from here in the first place.' No doubt what he meant was that the traveller had got on to the wrong road and would have to go back, but that is not what he said!

If you are going on a journey, you could see it as having three aspects – where you are coming from, where you are now, and where you want to get to. We could make a comparison with our own lives. Our life's journey has a starting point, and we are all at a certain point on the journey now. It is useful at times to look back on that journey and to try to analyse those things we are pleased with and those we are not. If we do this we will then be better able to plan out the next stages of the journey by building on experiences, both good and bad. It is also very useful to assess how you can be helped in the journey of life, and what contribution you can make to help others through their journeys.

School helps you learn the skills you need for the journey, and helps you use the experiences of the past to make a better future. From history, literature, religion and the arts, we gain an understanding of our culture and people's lives in this country and throughout the world; from geography, technology and the sciences, we are equipping ourselves with knowledge and understanding of our world; and, of course, we are using language, mathematical and physical skills in our everyday life. From all our studies, we should be gaining experiences that will help us to take our place in the world.

Friends also play an important role in our journey. We need friends to travel with us on life's journey. Sometimes we have things to give our friends; we can lend them a hand, or we can offer a friendly ear when they want to talk. At other times, we are the ones who need companionship and support. Friendship is sharing and caring, laughing and crying together, spending time with each other, learning from and with each other. There's a well-known proverb which says, 'A friend in need is a friend indeed'. It is in times of need, when the going gets tough, that we realize who our true friends are. They don't desert us when we most need their help; they are the people in whom we can trust.

Aesop was a Greek writer who lived over 2000 years ago. He wrote many short stories, usually known as fables. Like most good stories, each has an important message that is true for all times. Aesop's story of the Bear and the Travellers tells us a lot about true friendship.

Two travellers were on the road together, when a bear suddenly appeared on the scene. Before the bear spotted the travellers, one of them made for a tree at the side of the road, climbed up into the branches and hid there. The other was not so quick as his companion. Since he could not escape, he threw himself on the ground and pretended to be dead.

The bear came up and sniffed all round him, but the traveller kept perfectly still and held his breath. It is said that a bear will not touch a dead body. Luckily, the bear took him for a corpse and went away.

When the bear had disappeared, the traveller who had hid in the tree came down and asked his companion what the bear had whispered to him when he put his mouth to his ear. The other replied, 'He told me never again to travel with a friend who deserts you at the first sign of danger.'

We need our friends; our friends need us. Friends need to be able to rely on each other, and to feel that they will not be let down. We need the help and support of many people as we travel through life. In the earlier stages of the journey, school provides a vital part of this help and support. If we are open to the benefits to be derived from school, we will gain a great deal from our time there. With a positive attitude and with the encouragement of true friends, we will all have the strength to continue life's journey, confident that we know where we are going and how best to get there.

A PRAYER

✵

O God, help us to learn from experience and to establish our priorities for what we hope to achieve. May we value our friendships and not let our friends down.

Amen.

Making Mistakes

* Why we make mistakes
* The consequences of making mistakes
* Learning from our mistakes
* Learning humility and tolerance of others
* Jesus' advice on attitudes towards others

We all make mistakes at times, and it is worth considering why we do so. Sometimes we make an error because we are doing a routine job automatically without really thinking about it. For example, most people will make a pot of tea regularly. It is something that involves several different operations, but because it is done so often it becomes routine and most people will do it without much thought about what they are doing. You may start thinking about other things or perhaps just daydream. However, if you start daydreaming and doing a routine job automatically, you can easily make mistakes. If you leave out a stage in the tea-making operation, like pouring the water in the pot without putting the tea in, or if you repeat a stage, like filling the teapot twice, then the results will be rather unexpected! A mistake has been made but, in this example, there are no serious consequences.

Sometimes, however, simple mistakes can lead to disaster. In March 1977, the worst ever civil aircraft disaster occurred. In bad visibility at Tenerife Airport, two jumbo jets collided and 570 people were killed. The facts were simple: the Pan-Am jet didn't turn off the runway when taxi-ing towards the take-off point, and the KLM jet took off too soon. But why should such errors have been made?

The Pan-Am crew were preoccupied with listening to Air Traffic Control talking to the KLM crew; by concentrating on this, they missed the turning off the runway – this was the first mistake. The KLM crew were given instructions for preparing for take-off, but because the aircraft controller used the phrase 'take-off' this triggered off the familiar routine in the cockpit, and the captain started the plane down the runway. The Pan-Am crew heard the conversation about preparing for take-off and reminded Control that they were on the runway. The KLM crew didn't hear this, but they heard Control say 'OK' and started the process of the plane's gathering speed. The horrific crash was now inevitable.

Why should the KLM captain attempt to take off without clearance? Apparently, he had spent a lot of time training pilots in a simulator. When in the simulator, it was the practice to give clearance instructions, followed immediately by permission to take off. With all the other stresses, such as bad weather and the fact that he had worked long hours, he made the fatal mistake and assumed he could take off.

These examples illustrate that mistakes can be made for a number of reasons – lack of concentration, over-familiarity, or unusual or difficult circumstances. To avoid making mistakes, we need to take care, and we need to develop our skills so that we are better able to perform the tasks we have to face.

Of course we all make mistakes from time to time, but it is important to learn from our mistakes. It is also important to recognize our mistakes and to admit to them. If we don't admit to ourselves that we have made a mistake then we will not learn from our experience. Admitting one's errors is an important part of the quality of learning humility. We can also learn tolerance of others from our own mistakes. Next time someone makes a mistake that irritates you, think of the mistakes you yourself have made.

Jesus had some good advice to give on the subject of our own faults and our attitude to those of others, as this extract from St John's Gospel illustrates:

The doctors of the law and the Pharisees brought in a woman detected in adultery. Making her stand in the middle they said to him, 'Master, this woman was caught in the very act of adultery. In the Law Moses has laid down that such women are to be stoned. What do you say about it?' They put the question as a test, hoping to frame a charge against him. ... When they continued to press their question he sat up straight and said, 'That one of you who is faultless shall cast the first stone.' ... When they heard what he said, one by one they went away, the eldest first; and Jesus was left alone with the woman still standing there. Jesus said to the woman,

'Where are they? Has no one condemned you?' 'No one, sir', she said. *Jesus replied, 'No more do I. You may go; do not sin again.'*

(John 8:3–11)

'That one of you who is faultless shall cast the first stone.' None of us is faultless. We need to strive hard to learn from our mistakes and we need to learn tolerance of others.

A PRAYER

O God, teach us to show consideration to others whatever their strengths and weaknesses. Help us to recognize our own failings and errors, and give us the humility to learn from our mistakes so that we may be more understanding of others.

Amen.

A New Experience

* Describing new experiences to others
* Learning from experience
* Guidance from the world's religions
* Codes of behaviour
* Dependence on each other
* Distinguishing what is worthwhile from what is not

A large map of China could be displayed to show Marco Polo's journey. You might also want to have a lump of coal on display.

Learning from Experience

ne of the most difficult things to do is to try to describe to someone else something which you have experienced but which the other person has not. For example, how would you describe snow to someone from the tropics in such a way that that person would really understand what snow was like? It is equally difficult, if not more so, to describe an intense emotional experience to someone who has not had the same experience.

Listen to this extract written by Marco Polo, about 800 years ago. He is describing something he experienced in China which he had not encountered before, and which no one in his native Venice had encountered either.

Throughout China there is a sort of black stone, which they dig out of the mountains, where it runs in veins. When lighted, it burns like charcoal, and retains the fire much better than wood; insomuch that it may be preserved during the night, and in the morning be found still burning. These stones do not flame, excepting a little when first lighted, but during their ignition give out a considerable heat. It is true there is no scarcity of wood in the country, but the multitude of inhabitants is so immense, and the stoves, and baths, which they are continually heating, so numerous, that the quantity could not supply the demand; for there is no person who does not frequent the warm bath at least three times a week, and during the winter daily, if it is in their power. Every man of rank or wealth has one in his house for his own use; and the stock of wood must soon prove inadequate to such consumption; whereas these stones may be had in great abundance, and at a cheap rate.

That is, of course, a description of coal. We can recognize it because we know what coal is. Until quite recently, coal was part of everyday life for most people in this country. Although today far fewer people use coal, everyone knows what it is and what it's used for. However, to Venetians in the Middle Ages coal was unknown. They had no concept of coal, so Marco Polo needed to describe it in some detail. How did he set about doing so?

An important part of his description compares coal with something his readers will understand – wood. He also spends some time writing about the main use of coal – heating water for baths; again, this is something his readers will be familiar with. He is trying to extend their understanding by building on experiences with which they are already familiar. And that is what education is all about. It is providing new experiences, in an orderly way and based on previous experiences, to help the learner develop further.

And, of course, that's what life is all about. It doesn't happen so methodically, nor in such an orderly way, as in the classroom, but life is a process of extending experiences. Of course, in life, some experiences are good and some not so good. So how can we distinguish the good from the bad, the important from the trivial? It's often very difficult to know, and, of course, what's good in one situation may be bad in another. All people – young or old, simple or sophisticated – need models to guide them, and it is important to have a code of conduct as a basis for life. We may not necessarily agree with every detail in the code, but that is less important than the existence of broad principles which must be sound and coherent.

Traditionally the great religions of the world have provided moral codes as guidance for behaviour. We talk about the Christian way of life, for instance, or the Muslim way of life. What is remarkable is not the differences between the moral fundamentals of the great religions of the world, but the similarities between them. Inspiration for life can come from other sources as well. A great work of art, or literature, or music can raise human experience above the ordinary and lift a person to new heights. Inspiration may also come from the example of another person's life, whether it is a famous person or someone we know personally, like a friend or relative.

Our development as human beings is a complex process. Two of the greatest lessons we have to learn are the fact that we are all dependent on each other, and that we need to be able to distinguish what is worthwhile from what is not. We need the help and inspiration of examples to build on our experiences. The guidance given by the world's religions provides a basic framework for us and much of that framework is common to all religions. The Ten Commandments, given by God to Moses, are the basis of the Jewish religion. Here is a shortened version of them:

You shall have no other Gods except me.
You shall not make any idol for yourself.

You shall not misuse the name of God.
Remember to keep the sabbath day holy.
Honour your father and your mother.
You shall not commit murder.
You shall not commit adultery.
You shall not steal.
You shall not give false evidence.
You shall not covet things that are not yours.

(Adapted from Exodus 20:3–17)

A PRAYER

O God, give us the sense to build on experience, the insight to see what we should do, the courage to act upon it, and the conviction to continue on the right path.

Amen.

Building on Experience

✳ Dangers of wasting time
✳ Making the most of the present by learning from the past
✳ The sum of human experience: the 1953 Everest expedition
✳ Making progress is not failure

The assembly could start with a tape recording of some programme announcements and previews from radio or television. A large picture showing climbers tackling Everest or a similarly impressive peak could be displayed.

It's so easy to waste time; sometimes it's a way of delaying doing something we don't really want to do. It's not just individuals who waste time. Think of the amount of time spent by television channels showing clips of programmes to be broadcast later. It's done mainly to persuade us to continue viewing, but it takes up a lot of time that could be used on real programmes. Many of our favourite programmes could be five minutes longer were it not for all the bits and pieces in between. It's also a way of saving money since all these trivial fillers make cheap television time!

How can we avoid wasting time? How can we make sure that we live our lives fully? How can we get the most out of the present?

Part of the answer to these questions comes by looking at the past. We can learn a lot by looking at what we and others have done in the past, by learning from past mistakes, and by using the experience of the past to do things better in the future: in other words, to build on experience. That's what we are doing all the time, usually unconsciously, but at other times quite deliberately learning from the past. The critical factor is whether we successfully learn from experience – how to repair that bicycle puncture successfully, how to do the science experiment properly, how to get on better with that person you don't really like. We need to learn from our experiences and, of course, from the experiences of others. Sir John Hunt led the first successful expedition to climb Mount Everest. This is what he said about it:

> *What were the reasons for our success? How was it that we succeeded in getting to the top when so many before us had failed to do so? I am adding the second question only to give what, in my mind, is the one reason transcending all others which explains the first. For I wish once again to pay tribute to the work of earlier expeditions.*
>
> *The significance of all these other attempts is that, regardless of the height they reached, each one added to the mounting sum of experience, and this experience had to reach a certain total before the riddle could be solved. The building of this pyramid of experience was vital to the whole issue; only when it had attained a certain height was it within the power of any team of mountaineers to fashion its apex. Seen in this light, other expeditions did not fail; they made progress. They had reached this stage when we prepared to try again last winter. By that time, but not before, the defences by which the mountain had so*

far withstood assault were well enough known; it only remained to study them and draw the right conclusions in order to launch yet one more party which would have every weapon – material and human – with which to do battle against Everest. We of the 1953 Everest Expedition are proud to share the glory with our predecessors.

Above all, and independent of their lessons, we were inspired by their example, their persistence, their spirit of quest, their determination that there should be no surrender. For this compelling urge to continue the struggle, we have above all else to thank the earlier Everest climbers.

Since 1953, more and more groups – large and small – have successfully climbed Everest; indeed, today, the world's most experienced climbers look elsewhere for their ultimate challenges. But all who have tackled Everest since 1953 have also, in their turn, learned from the experiences of those who went before them. In that sense, Sir John Hunt's expedition was only one in the totality of experiences that today's climbers call upon.

There is one particularly significant sentence in Sir John Hunt's account: 'Other expeditions did not fail; they made progress.' That is an important factor in our lives as well. We shall not reach the climax of our lives today; we shall not do everything perfectly. But we should try to do everything as best we can. We need to learn from the past to make more progress today. We need to remember that today's present is tomorrow's past. Tomorrow we may learn something from what has happened today. So we need to make the experience of today, and every day, worth remembering.

A PRAYER

O God, help us to know that which is worth knowing, to love
that which is worth loving, to praise that which can bear praise,
and to prize that which is precious.

Amen.

Development and Progress

> ❋ Development of the railway locomotive as an example of building on experience
> ❋ Learning from our own and others' experience
> ❋ Striving for progress and using our opportunities
>
> This assembly uses the development of the railway engine as an example of its theme. A series of posters, or overhead transparencies or slides, showing the development of that or any other form of transport, could be displayed around the room.

Museums are fascinating places and can give us an insight into many aspects of the past. There are a number of specialist transport museums, many of which provide opportunities to ride on the transport on display. At the National Tramways Museum at Crich in Derbyshire, for example, you can ride on the mile-long track from the terminus in a re-created Victorian street to the other end out in the countryside. At Duxford in Cambridgeshire is a vast aircraft museum which combines indoor exhibits with a large display of aircraft of different ages and types, many of which are open to view; periodically, there are air shows, and it is possible to go on short demonstration flights. One of the finest transport museums is the National Railway Museum in York; here you can trace the development of railways and locomotives from the beginning of the railway age right up to the building of the Channel Tunnel. Let's look very briefly at the development of the railway locomotive.

The railway engine or locomotive is a moving machine that runs on smooth rails to pull passenger carriages or freight. It is a very efficient and safe means of transport and has made great progress since its introduction nearly 200 years ago. Over time, the design of railway engines changed as modifications and improvements were introduced

Learning from Experience

in the light of experience. In the National Railway Museum you can see examples of different engines built over the years. Though their purpose is the same, you cannot mistake the old ones for the new ones. It is fairly easy to place the engines in order of age. Designers and engineers have learned from past mistakes and from experience, and progress has been made.

When the 150th anniversary of the opening of the first railway was celebrated in 1975, a procession of locomotives took place to show the development of the railway engine over this period. The procession was led by a replica of the original 1825 'Locomotion' steam engine built by George Stephenson, with British Rail's High Speed Train, which holds the world speed record for diesel traction, bringing up the rear. At the National Railway Museum, you can see 'The Rocket', built in 1830 and already improved from the 'Locomotion', and the whole development of the railway engine up to the most modern designs for Channel Tunnel traffic. The story of the railway engine is one of continuous development.

The story of human life has similarities to the development of the railway engine. You start off with a good idea – a new human being, a baby – and she or he develops from there. It is fairly easy to pick out the stages in development as the person learns from experience and mistakes, as well as from the advice of others who are more experienced. Some railway engines were more successful than others because their designers more skilfully used the available knowledge and experience. Similarly, human beings will be more successful if they learn from experience and use the opportunities available to them. In the development of the railway engine, certain ideas were not successful and simply led up blind alleys. We must strive to ensure that the choices we make do not lead us up blind alleys, but take us forward as we make full use of all the opportunities open to us.

Museums can be useful as reminders of the ways in which development occurs. They can also show us what may happen if things go wrong. It is worthwhile to compare our own development with that of the aircraft, the motor car or the railway engine and ask ourselves whether we are satisfied with the progress we have made, whether there is room for improvement and whether there is potential for further development.

A PRAYER

✿

O God, make us aware of our dependence on others and of the opportunities open to us. Help us to grasp those opportunities so that our lives are continuously developing in ways that contribute to positive progress for ourselves and others.

Amen.

Learning from Experience

4

Living in the Community

Courtesy, Consideration and Co-operation

* Living in a community
* The 'Three Cs' as the key to behaviour in a civilized community
* 'The whole is greater than the sum of its parts'
* St Paul's analogy with the body

The theme of this assembly is appropriate at any time, but perhaps particularly so at the start of a school year or term. After the introduction, the meaning of the three 'C's could be read by three pupils.

Our school is a community in which we have to learn to live with others. All of us live in different communities in different situations, but the school community is of great importance to those who are part of it. How successfully people fit into their communities will depend to a large extent on how well they learn to live with those around them.

The word 'community' begins with the letter 'C'. Three other words beginning with 'C' are useful ones to remember if we are to live successfully in a community. These words are 'courtesy', 'consideration' and 'co-operation'.

Courtesy means having respect for others. In a school it means respect for teachers and what they are doing, and it means respect for other pupils, their ideas, their views and their personalities – even if you don't like them very much. It may be that there are others who don't much like you!

Consideration means thinking of others before yourself. It is so easy to rush down a corridor or a staircase with a friend and barely notice a small pupil, or perhaps a disabled pupil, coming the other way. It may be amusing to make a nuisance of yourself in class, or elsewhere, because you are bored, but you are spoiling everything for others. So, be considerate of others – young people and adults alike.

Co-operation is necessary if we are to get the most from life at school. We must work with each other, not against each other. Working with each other is what the word 'co-operation' means, and we should expect everyone to co-operate in the school community.

The 'Three Cs' should influence how everyone behaves in the school community. Courtesy towards others, consideration for others, co-operation with others. Both teachers and pupils should demonstrate these things so that everyone can play their full part in the community and contribute to the life of the school. You may know the phrase 'The whole is greater than the sum of its parts'. Mathematically that may be incorrect, but in terms of human achievement it is true indeed.

St Paul compared a community to a human body, with each part of the body having an important role to play. Without any one part, the body is incomplete. So it is with a community; each member has a part to play and without any member the community is incomplete. Everyone is important and should be treated with respect, and, of course, everyone depends on one another to make the community work. This is what St Paul said:

A body is not a single organ, but many. Suppose the foot should say, 'Because I am not a hand, I do not belong to the body', it does belong to the body none the less. Suppose the ear were to say, 'Because I am not an eye, I do not belong to the body', it still does belong to the body. If the body were all eye, how could it hear? If the body were all ear, how could it smell? But, in fact, God appointed each limb and organ to its own place in the body as he chose. If the whole were one single organ, there would not be a body at all; in fact, however, there are many different organs, but one body. The eye cannot say to the hand, 'I do not need you'; nor the head to the feet, 'I do not need you.' Quite the contrary: those organs of the body which seem to be more frail than the others are indispensable, and those parts of the body which we regard as less honourable are treated with special honour. To our unseemly parts is given a more than ordinary seemliness, whereas our seemly parts need no special adorning. But God has combined the various parts of the body, giving special honour to the humbler parts, so that there might be no sense of division in the body, but that all its organs might feel the same concern for one another. If one organ suffers, they all suffer together. If one flourishes, they all rejoice together.

(1 Corinthians 12:14–26)

Remember the 'Three Cs' as the key to living in a civilized community – and there we have two more 'C's. We are all important in our community. We should help one another when difficulties arise, and, equally, we should celebrate success and achievement when they occur. So the equation for our behaviour can be:

Courtesy + Consideration + Co-operation = Civilized Community

---

A PRAYER

O God, we thank you for all the benefits that living in the school community can bring. We pray that all of us will practise courtesy, consideration and co-operation so that all members may share equally in the completeness of a civilized community.

Amen.

The Use of Language

* Changing use of words
* The richness of language and the abuse of language
* The value of words in communicating
* St Paul's message to the Corinthians about the gift of love

One of the most precious gifts that human beings possess is the gift of language. The ability to use words is something that not only distinguishes us from the rest of the living world, but enables us to communicate our thoughts and ideas to each other.

Today we are going to look very briefly at three aspects of the use of words: first, the way in which the use of words can change over time; secondly, the beauty and richness of the English language; and thirdly, the use of words to convey meaning and ideas.

We all know of words that have become old-fashioned or even changed their meaning over the years. Sometimes this happens slowly, sometimes quite quickly. None of us would now, in everyday speech, use words like 'thou' and 'thee'. 'Thou art a silly fool' doesn't ring true now, but a few hundred years ago it would have been the way of speaking. Sometimes the meanings of words can change very quickly. For instance, to describe someone as 'gay' now conveys an entirely different meaning from that of a few years ago.

A number of years ago, one of the police forces in this country built a new headquarters. But they wanted to change the name of the road where their new building was situated. This might seem surprising because many road names are very ancient and often of historical interest. Indeed the name of the road gave a clue to its original use. Why should the police want to destroy this link with the past? Well, the road was called Pig Lane. Unfortunately, the word 'pig' has become a word of abuse for the police, and, at the time of this event in the 1970s, the new use of the word was a sufficiently sensitive issue for the police to want to change the name, though previously it had conveyed quite a different meaning.

Living in the Community

The English language contains thousands and thousands of words, many of them very beautiful. The range of words is enormous. The French may insist that their language is more subtle and refined, and the Germans may claim that their language is more forceful, but English has enormous variety. It is regrettable, therefore, to hear people use swear words as part of their everyday language. Some people seem to accept swearing as normal speech. But really they are saying something about their poverty – the poverty of their language. When the language is so rich, why devalue it, and ourselves, by a monotonous and restricted use of words? It is also an insult to those who have to listen, because it is, in fact, an abuse of the language.

But words are worthless unless they are used to communicate, and, obviously, it is the quality of the message that gives words their true significance. Words can be used in a way that makes no sense, or to convey only a trivial message, or they can be used in a way that is important and significant.

The reading from one of St Paul's letters illustrates the three aspects of language that we're looking at. First, it illustrates the change in the meaning of words. The key word in this passage in the seventeenth-century Authorized Version of the Bible has been changed in more modern translations. The key word is 'charity'. Today, the word 'charity' has a meaning and a use that is quite different from that of 400 years ago. So modern translations use the word 'love' rather than 'charity'. If anyone read the old version without realizing the change in meaning, the passage would convey a completely different idea; although some people might argue that the word 'love' is now overused and doesn't convey the depth of meaning that St Paul intended.

Secondly, the passage is one of great beauty and illustrates the richness of the language, particularly when read aloud. And, finally, the meaning conveyed by the words has something to say to all of us. St Paul's message about the great gift of love is so strong that the reading can stand by itself without further comment.

If I speak in the tongues of men and of angels, but have not love, I am only a resounding gong or a clashing cymbal. If I have the gift of prophecy and can fathom all mysteries and all knowledge, and if I have a faith that can move mountains, but have not love, I am nothing. If I give all that I possess to the poor and surrender my body to the flames, but have not love, I gain nothing.

Love is patient, love is kind. It does not envy, it does not boast, it is not proud. It is not rude, it is not self-seeking, it is not easily angered, it keeps no record of wrongs. Love does not delight in evil but rejoices with the truth. It always protects, always trusts, always hopes, always perseveres.

Love never fails. But where there are prophecies, they will cease; where there are tongues, they will be stilled; where there is knowledge, it will pass away. For we know in part and we prophesy in part, but when perfection comes, the imperfect disappears. When I was a child, I talked like a child, I thought like a child, I reasoned like a child. When I became a man, I put away childish ways behind me. Now we see but a poor reflection, as in a mirror; then, we shall see face to face. Now I know in part; then I shall know fully, even as I am fully known.

And now these three remain: faith, hope and love. But the greatest of these is love.

(1 Corinthians 13)

A PRAYER

O God, help us to live together in love and peace, patient with each other's faults and mindful of each other's needs. May we use words with thought and good sense, so that we convey a message of love, not seeking what is good for ourselves only, but what is for the good of all.

Amen.

Living in the Community

Perceptions of Truth

✳ Different interpretations of the same thing
✳ What is truth? – from Pilate to company boardrooms
✳ How can we seek the truth?
✳ Honesty and sympathy towards others

Ideally, the drawing, familiar to Gestalt psychology, needs to be shown on an overhead transparency. If this is not possible, an enlarged version could be held up and subsequently displayed on a notice-board so that those who are interested can study it at leisure.

There is a well-known drawing that is sometimes used by psychologists who analyse shapes and patterns. When some people look at it, they see a side view of a beautiful young girl with a ribbon around her neck. When others look at it, they see a wrinkled old lady with a bent nose, wearing a shawl. And yet they are looking at the same drawing – exactly the same lines on the drawing. What you see depends on the way you look at the drawing, and the way your eyes focus on it; it depends on your perception of the drawing. It is also interesting to learn that, even when the alternative interpretation is pointed out, most people continue to focus on their original perception, whatever that was.

So here is a situation where the same thing can be interpreted in two completely different ways. The facts are the same, but the understanding or the perception of them is quite different. Indeed, the truth is not always easy to establish. There is a well-known passage in St John's Gospel when, just before he was crucified, Jesus was being questioned by Pilate.

'You are a king, then?' said Pilate.
Jesus answered, '"King" is your word. My task is to bear witness to the truth. For this I was born; for this I came into the world, and all who are not deaf to truth listen to my voice.'
Pilate said, 'What is truth?'

(John 18:37–38)

•••

What indeed is truth? Jesus was talking about the truth in understanding life itself. But, even at a much simpler level, it is not always easy to establish the truth. How many times has every teacher tried to establish the truth in an argument between pupils? 'It's not my fault. He started it.' 'No, I didn't. She started it.'

It is not just amongst children that different versions of the truth arise. In industry and commerce, conflicting interpretations of the facts are common. In cases where one company wants to take over another and a vote of shareholders is necessary to decide whether the takeover will proceed, both sides will often spend thousands of pounds on advertisements urging shareholders to vote one way or the other. Somewhere in such advertisements, usually in small print at the bottom, you will read words like 'This advertisement is published by The Black Rock Company plc, whose directors have taken all reasonable care to ensure that the facts stated and the opinions expressed herein are fair and accurate'. A day or two later, an advertisement from the The White Rock Company plc, urging shareholders to take the opposite view, will contain a similar sentence from its directors, claiming that their advertisement is also fair and accurate. The facts are the same, but the interpretation is different. What is the truth?

Politicians from different political parties are renowned for the way that they argue opposing views and interpretations from apparently the same facts. So, if company directors and politicians interpret facts in completely different ways, how can we seek the truth in matters that affect us?

Of course, it is not easy and clearly people will always have genuine differences of opinion. All of us will have our own ways of trying to search for the truth in our lives. Some will look to their religious beliefs to find inspiration in the search for truth. But there are some qualities that should be common to all of us.

One vital ingredient in the search for truth is honesty – honesty with ourselves and honesty in our dealings with others. We should not say one thing to one person and another thing to someone else. We should not mislead people or pretend to be what we are not. Another quality is sympathy towards others. Of course, we do not like everyone; we may have little in common with many people and may not like their lifestyles. But we can still treat them with dignity and respect, and show sympathy as fellow human beings.

Throughout our lives we will have differences of opinion with other people and our perceptions and understanding of the facts may sometimes be different from those of others. But, if we search for the truth with honesty and with sympathy towards others, we will be contributing to human life as a whole.

A PRAYER

O God, help us through our perceptions of life to search for the truth in everything we do. Give us honesty and sympathy towards others so that our search will lead to a greater understanding of the purposes of life.

Amen.

Hope and Despair

✳ Causes of crime
✳ Rights and responsibilities
✳ The relationship between individuals and society
✳ Overcoming despair by being positive

A number of police posters that convey an anti-crime message, preferably incorporating the importance of social responsibility, could be displayed during the assembly.

Listen to this quotation from a newspaper:

A 38-year-old woman stopped her car to allow two young men to push their vehicle, which appeared to have stalled, across the road.

They tied her up in the back of her own car with a plastic bag over her head, sexually assaulted her during a 2 hour drive, doused her and the car in inflammable liquid, and left her in the back of the burning vehicle. By a miracle she escaped before her clothes caught fire.

What is your reaction to that story? Is it typical of our society today? Why did those men do such a horrifying thing? What can we do to stop crimes like this? What are the causes of crime?

Fortunately crimes like the one just described are rare. Those two young men showed an utter heartlessness and ruthlessness that is a result of total alienation from society. Such people are unable to relate to other people and treat them as objects. They are unable to distinguish between right and wrong, or, if capable of distinguishing, they choose wrong. The causes of crime are complex and many people disagree on what are the most significant factors.

Sometimes crime originates in stupid behaviour without thought about the consequences. A police campaign against shoplifting by young people once used the slogan 'What starts as a game will end in shame'. This particular campaign was aimed at raising awareness that shoplifting is theft, and that theft has serious consequences for anyone who is caught. Those who are regular criminals come from many backgrounds and circumstances. Although some criminals come from broken, violent or unloving homes, the majority of people from such homes are not criminals. Poverty and unemployment may help to breed crime, but only a tiny minority views crime as a solution. Many criminals are, in material terms, well off. Undoubtedly, much crime today is directly or indirectly related to drug abuse, as addicts resort to crime to pay for their habit.

There is no easy answer to problems of crime and other forms of anti-social behaviour. Crime may arise from despair and its effects can easily cause despair. If there is despair, there can be no hope. When people face enormous problems it is very difficult to feel positive. But the need to be positive is vital and we must be prepared to state clearly the values and principles we believe in. The relationship between the individual and society is a very important one. We have rights as individuals, but we also have duties that go hand-in-hand with those rights. The responsibilities of individuals and the community complement each other. We cannot exist in a world where no one takes responsibility for their actions. If we do not learn the difference between right and wrong and live our lives accordingly, then the result is chaos.

A useful way of summarizing a positive code of behaviour is to remember the 'Three Cs' – courtesy towards others, consideration for others and co-operation with others. We could also list three negative things, the 'Three Vs' – violence, vandalism and verbal abuse. When things go wrong, the cause is often one or more of these three. If we aim for the 'Three Cs' and stand up against the 'Three Vs' then we shall have a positive society – a society where everyone is treated with respect, whatever their age, sex, race, ability or circumstances.

None of this is easy to achieve, and when you look at some aspects of our society, both today and in past generations, it is tempting to say, 'What's the point?' But don't! We need to show the way, all of us, through our individual lives. If we believe in the values and principles of a positive society, there will be hope and not despair.

A PRAYER

O God, we pray for those who can see no hope, for those who are in despair, and for those who believe that society has nothing for them. We pray also for the victims of crime and those who suffer as a result of crime. Help all of us to value what is right and discard what is wrong, so that we contribute to our world in a positive way.

Amen.

People Matter:
an Example from Africa

> ✳ Ignoring the needs of people – the example of an
>   agricultural development project
> ✳ Importance of sensitivity to people's needs
>
> A map of Africa to show the position of Sierra Leone would
> be helpful. To introduce some variety, the five examples of
> what went wrong could be read or talked about by five
> different people. The leader then has the role of
> introducing, linking together and concluding the assembly.

If you look at a map of Africa, you will see a small country on the west coast called Sierra Leone. Its population is less than half that of London. Its main food product is rice, but by the 1970s not enough was being grown to feed the population and quite a large sum of money was being spent each year on rice imports. This was money that the country could scarcely afford to spend.

An agricultural development project was set up. Much of the money for this at first came from the World Bank, one of whose aims is to help developing countries. The project sounded like a planner's dream. The scheme would allow more rice to be produced so fewer imports would be necessary. It would make the country areas more prosperous and would stop people moving to the capital, Freetown, which couldn't cope with the influx of people. Previously unproductive swamp land would be used to grow swamp rice, so pressure on the land would be eased.

It sounded like an excellent scheme, but, to understand things fully, it is necessary to realize that there are two main types of rice – hill rice and swamp rice. Hill rice grows on slopes; it is the traditional type of rice grown in Sierra Leone. The problem is that the land could be used for rice only for about two years and then it had to be left for four years to regain its fertility. Swamp rice grows on swamp land. The fields

Living in the Community

are covered in water for much of the time and a crop can be grown each year, particularly if fertilizers are used. It was swamp rice production that was to be encouraged in the development project because the yields from swamp rice would be about three times those from hill rice.

The scheme started in the early 1970s. It seemed to be a great success. Within two years, all the planned areas in the pilot scheme were in use; the idea was that the farmers in these areas would then teach other farmers the new methods so that the scheme would spread. Yields of rice from the swamp lands were indeed more than double the hill rice yields. But then things started going badly wrong. Why? There were a number of reasons, of which the following were probably the most significant.

First, swamp rice yields could be maintained only by using fertilizers. For the first two years there was a subsidy on the fertilizers. Then the subsidy was removed and, with price rises as well, the cost of fertilizers more than doubled. Many farmers couldn't afford to fertilize their land and, consequently, yields fell.

Secondly, growing swamp rice needs a lot of labour and most of the work occurs at certain times of the year. With hill rice, the farmers and their families could do all the work themselves because it was spread out fairly evenly over the year, but with swamp rice, the farmers had to hire expensive labour to cope with the concentration of work during the busy periods.

Another problem was the fact that the planners had concentrated only on rice. Certainly rice yields were improved, but on swamp land only rice can be grown. It didn't occur to the planners that a diet of rice alone is a bit monotonous. The uplands could produce a wider range of food because other things as well as rice could be grown.

Furthermore, it soon became obvious that the people did not like swamp rice. They found hill rice more satisfying and liked the taste of it better. It is rather like saying to you that you can't eat bread from now on, but it doesn't matter because you can eat spaghetti instead. Spaghetti and bread are both made from wheat, so there won't be any difference. That's no good, though, if you like bread but don't like spaghetti!

There were many other reasons why things went wrong, but one more will be sufficient to illustrate the difficulties. As in so many farming areas like Sierra Leone, much of the work in the fields is done by women; the cooking is also done by women. If the women are busy in the fields, they haven't much time for cooking. Now hill rice can be cooked, say, in the morning for a meal, and then what's not used straight away can be heated up again later and still taste very good. That doesn't work with swamp rice, so it was very unpopular with the cooks.

None of these problems came into the calculations of the planners. The idea of agricultural development in Sierra Leone based on swamp rice has been a dream which has faded away, because the planners did not understand or take into account the most important element in the scheme – people. The plan was directed at the product – rice – and not the producer – the people.

There's a lesson for everyone here – in Britain as much as in Sierra Leone. Consideration of the needs of people is vitally important. In the last forty or so years in Britain, probably the classic example of product- rather than people-based thinking has been the building of vast, multi-storey blocks of flats. The emphasis was on using the least amount of land for the greatest number of housing units rather than on considering the sort of housing that people wanted.

In our own daily lives, as much as in large-scale planning decisions, we must not ignore or forget the fact that we are all human beings, with an important part to play in the world around us. It is vital that we are always sensitive to the needs of others and that we constantly endeavour to understand one another.

A PRAYER

✪

O God, give us thoughtfulness, imagination and patience to discover why people feel and think and behave as they do, so that our understanding may grow and our sympathy may deepen.

Amen.

5

Ideals and Equality

Martin Luther and Martin Luther King

* The life of Martin Luther and his part in the Reformation
* The life of Martin Luther King and civil rights in the U.S.A.
* Standing up for one's beliefs
* Discrimination and prejudice
* Peaceful protest

With some planning, there are possibilities for dramatizing the two stories in this assembly. The selling of indulgences by unscrupulous priests to gullible peasants could be acted out, as could an example of racial discrimination in the American South. If there is sufficient time, a longer extract from Martin Luther King's speech could be read.

Well over 400 years and the Atlantic Ocean separate the German Martin Luther and the twentieth-century American Martin Luther King. The parents of the American named their son after the German monk who changed the course of European history. Martin Luther King has been one of the most influential figures in twentieth-century America. Both men will always have a place in history because they stood up for the things they believed to be important.

Ideals and Equality

Martin Luther lived from 1483 to 1546. For many years he was an unknown German monk, but by the end of his life he was a famous person – notorious to many – whose actions were in the vanguard of the great religious upheavals of the period that is called the Reformation, and he was branded as a heretic by the Catholic Church.

Why did the course of Luther's life change so much? The main reason was that he fought against what he believed was wrong in the religion of his time. He fought against what he saw as the corruption of the Church and the way it used the fears and superstitions of simple people for its own ends. He did this in a peaceful way by stating what he believed was right. The particular evil he attacked was what was known as the Doctrine of Indulgences. An indulgence was a piece of paper signed by the Pope which was supposed to take away sins in return for payment of money. In other words, if you bought an indulgence you might be saved from going to Hell – quite an attractive idea to a simple fifteenth-century peasant. More than that, some said that you could buy indulgences to help relatives who had already died: you could relieve their suffering in Hell or Purgatory and raise them to Heaven.

It is easy to imagine the trade that could be generated by unscrupulous priests carrying worthless pieces of paper, preying on the fears of ordinary people. Vast amounts of money were extracted from gullible people who made real sacrifices in the belief that the money they handed over would save them from their sins.

Luther preached that faith in Jesus Christ was the only way that people could redeem their sins. He attacked the doctrine of Indulgences and the corruption that went with it, and this brought him into conflict with the authority of the Pope. Luther's views and actions received much support, not least from ordinary people. The movement he started gathered momentum and led to the establishment of reformed or Protestant churches in many parts of the world. It also led to reforms within the Catholic Church.

Several centuries later, in a very different part of the world, another man fought for what he believed to be right against what he saw to be wrong. This man was the Reverend Martin Luther King. He was born in 1929 in the south of the United States where, despite the abolition of slavery long before his time, the black population was denied basic rights and was unable to enjoy the opportunities open to white American citizens. He fought for all people to have equal civil rights and to be treated with equal justice and he fought against the injustice caused by racial prejudice and segregation. He always advocated non-violence in his campaigning. In August 1963 he made a famous speech in which he spoke of his dream of the day when the American nation would treat all people equally. In the speech he said, 'I have a dream that my four little children will one day live in a nation where they will not be judged by the colour of their skin but by the content of their character'. His speech ended with these words:

From every mountainside, let freedom ring, and when this happens, when we allow freedom to ring, when we allow it to ring from every village and every hamlet, from every state and every city, we shall be able to speed up that day when all God's children, black and white, Jews and Gentiles, Protestants and Catholics, will be able to join hands and sing in the words of the old Negro spiritual, 'Free at last! Free at last! Thank God almighty, we are free at last!'

Martin Luther King received the Nobel Peace Prize in 1964 for his commitment to non-violent action for civil rights. When he was as-sassinated in 1968 he had much work still to do. However, much of the progress made by black people in the United States has been due to the work of Martin Luther King.

Both Martin Luther and Martin Luther King fought for what they believed was right. But they were fighting for causes – they were men of peace. They believed that through faith and hope, and through their words, they could succeed in achieving their aims: their methods were not violent but peaceful. Regrettably, theirs and so many other causes have become involved in violence. During the period of the Reformation, Europe became entangled in a number of wars in which the name of religion was used as an excuse for violent conflict. There has been much blood spilled by people with opposing views on civil rights in the United States and in many other parts of the world. Many others as well as Martin Luther King have been killed in the struggles.

Martin Luther and Martin Luther King stood up for their beliefs. They were committed to peace and they cared for other people. In thinking about their lives, we can reflect on the ways in which we can all contribute towards making the world a better and more peaceful place.

A PRAYER

O God, we pray that all people may enjoy justice and equal rights so that all can live in peace with dignity. May we gain inspiration from people like Martin Luther and Martin Luther King so that we may stand up for the principles of fairness and justice in a non-violent way.

Amen.

Freedom

* ✳ Human rights
* ✳ Free speech
* ✳ Steve Biko and Cry Freedom – the struggle for freedom in South Africa
* ✳ Accepting restrictions in order to create greater freedom
* ✳ Compulsory schooling – a restriction on freedom?
* ✳ The Christian concept of 'perfect freedom'

This assembly attempts to tackle a difficult concept and to emphasize the positive aspects of freedom. An opportunity for quiet reflection after the talk might be helpful, and an appropriate piece of music for this would be Sibelius' 'Finlandia'. Written in 1898 when Finland's struggle for freedom from the oppressive Tsarist empire was at its height, the music came to represent the culture and traditions of the Finnish people as they strove for independence.

'Freedom' is a word that is frequently used, sometimes coupled with the phrase 'human rights'. Indeed, people often talk of freedom as something that is everyone's right and the removal of someone's freedom as the worst possible thing that can happen. The importance of 'free speech' is often stressed. At times of elections, much is made of democratic rights and the 'freedom to decide our own future'. In parts of the world where democracy does not exist, people who campaign for equal rights for all are sometimes called 'freedom fighters'.

We must be careful, however, about the use of this word. Of course, if someone is put in prison they are deprived of their freedom to live an independent life and that is a serious matter. If people are slaves they are not free to do the sorts of things we take for granted. Some of you may have seen the film or read the book called *Cry Freedom*. They are based on two factual books about the true story of Steve Biko, a young black political leader in South Africa in the 1970s, who struck up a friendship with a white newspaper editor, Donald Woods. Both were passionately committed to ending what they saw as the oppression of the black majority population in South Africa. Biko died in controversial circumstances in police custody, and Woods fled from South Africa in order to write his books about these events. *Cry Freedom* tells the story of the two men and their fight for the freedom of black people in South Africa.

But what is 'freedom'? Is it the right to do whatever you like? Of course, it isn't. There is no such thing as absolute freedom. Absolute freedom – everyone doing exactly what they like – creates the opposite of freedom, that is anarchy or chaos. If drivers, for example, had absolute freedom on the roads, no one would get anywhere because life would be too dangerous. If everyone had the freedom to hit others over the head with iron bars, we would live in a country of fear; the strongest might survive, but life would be miserable for everyone. We all recognize this; we all know that there must be limits to freedom, that there must be rules. The difficulty is in defining what restrictions are necessary and acceptable, whom they are to be applied to, and how they are to be enforced.

The most important consideration is that freedom must be positive. It must be freedom to do something. We accept restrictions on our freedom in order to create greater freedom. We are not free to drive on the right-hand side of the road in order to create the greater freedom of being able to drive safely. We are not free to hit people over the head with iron bars so that we have the greater freedom of living without fear of attack. We accept that there have to be many restrictions, so the question we should ask is whether, by accepting these restrictions, we are able to enjoy greater opportunities, both as individuals and as members of society. It is important to remember that we are all members of society because that means that we have obligations as well as rights. If you are a member of a sports team, you accept restrictions on where you play and how you play in order to contribute to the team effort: it is the same with our membership of society as a whole.

One of the most significant restrictions that is imposed on all young people is the period of compulsory education. For eleven years, from the ages of five to sixteen, young people have no choice about what they do for considerable periods of time – the time spent at school. There have no doubt been times when many of you have thought, 'Oh, to be free of school'. If you had been young more than a hundred years ago, you may well have been free of the restrictions of having to go to school. But would you have been free? Your freedom has been restricted in order to give you the greater freedom of having more control over your life as an adult.

So we come back to the earlier questions. What restrictions are acceptable? What restrictions are not acceptable? Surely the key is to try to create a society in which people willingly accept codes of behaviour and ways of living that make a better society for everyone to enjoy. Restrictions are accepted because they are seen to be fair and just, and to contribute to the good of society as a whole.

Christians have a phrase that sums this up: 'In your service is perfect freedom'. That doesn't seem to make sense at first. If you are a servant of someone, you are not free; so how can perfect freedom come from being in someone's service? What Christians understand the phrase to mean is that if you follow the example of Christ, you are shown the way to lead a worthwhile life. In Christ's service you enjoy the benefits of following the example of a perfect person. Other religions provide similar ideals for us to follow. Whether or not you see it in religious terms, it is essential to understand the importance of having a code of behaviour for your life based on the need for society to have rules. We must accept that restrictions on personal liberty are necessary so that greater freedom is created for all to enjoy. If we respect the rights of others, we are all free to enjoy the benefits of living in a civilized society.

A PRAYER

O God, help us to be mindful of the needs of others so that we balance our personal freedom with the greater freedom that comes from living co-operatively within the wider community. We ask that those whose freedoms have been unjustly denied may be helped to secure what is their due so that they have the opportunity to live in a fair society.

Amen.

Reconciliation in South Africa

✳ The effects of apartheid
✳ The life and influence of Nelson Mandela
✳ The 'miracle' of democracy in South Africa
✳ The importance of reconciliation
✳ The need to work together in unity

Although it could be used at any time, this assembly would be particularly appropriate on or around 20th March (Human Rights Day in South Africa) or 10th May (the anniversary of Nelson Mandela's inauguration as President of South Africa). A large map of South Africa could be displayed and some of the important features and places pointed out.

For much of the twentieth century, the vast majority of the population of South Africa was denied basic human rights and justice. South Africa symbolized the evils of repression and the

Ideals and Equality

domination of the minority of the population over the majority on the basis of race and colour. For over forty years from 1948, the policy of 'apartheid', meaning 'separate development', was enforced by the South African Government. The policy was designed to prevent the mixing of black and white people and to ensure the continuing concentration of political and economic power in the hands of the white population which made up a good deal less than 20 per cent of the total. For many years, public buildings, railway carriages and even seats in parks displayed notices that said 'For whites only'. Blacks were forced to live in separate areas, and, to this day, many live in squalid conditions without adequate facilities in vast 'townships' that surround South Africa's cities. Educational, medical and other provisions for blacks were greatly inferior to those provided for whites.

The inevitable consequence of years of oppression and denial of opportunity to take part in the development of their country was the growth of protests as the black population struggled to assert itself. The African National Congress was dedicated to the overthrow of white minority rule, and bitter conflict became commonplace as the Government, through the police and the armed forces, clashed with the forces of the A.N.C. and other groups from the black population. One infamous example occurred on 20th March 1960, when sixty-nine black protesters were shot dead by police at Sharpeville, a black township on the edge of Cape Town. South Africa became increasingly isolated by the rest of the world. It left the British Commonwealth and many countries refused to trade with South Africa and imposed sanctions in an attempt to persuade the Government to change its policies. Meanwhile conflict and bloodshed continued and many people, both inside and outside South Africa, despaired of the future.

Throughout the period from the 1960s, one of the most influential leaders of the black population was Nelson Mandela. For his opposition to apartheid, he was exiled from South Africa, and then, in 1967, he was imprisoned for twenty-three years. Despite that, his influence, and the respect in which he was held, led the President of South Africa to begin to discuss with him alternative ways forward for the country. In February 1990 Nelson Mandela was released from prison and a new and more hopeful period in South Africa's history looked possible. However, few people could have hoped or imagined then that events would move so quickly that in four years' time the first elections would take place in which all South Africans of all races could vote, and that, on 10th May 1994, Nelson Mandela would be sworn in as the first President of a democratic South Africa.

The ceremony was impressive and the event passed off peacefully. It was attended by forty-two Heads of State and many leaders from all around the world. After all the oppression, all the conflict and bloodshed, one commentator described the elections and the events culminating in Nelson Mandela's installation as President as 'miraculous', a view echoed by the Queen when she visited South Africa a year later. A lot of the credit for this 'miracle' rests with Nelson Mandela and the previous President, F.W. de Klerk, who took the initiative in the process, but the coming of democracy is only the beginning and a tremendous responsibility lies with President Mandela and those who now have power in the country.

The difficulties in the years ahead will be immense. However, Nelson Mandela has repeatedly said that reconciliation is the only way forward for all parties and communities, regardless of colour, race or religion, if peace in South Africa is to be real. The path of violence is a totally unacceptable alternative. For many, one of the most memorable parts of the inauguration day was a spectacular 'fly past' of aircraft of South Africa's armed forces; it was the most symbolic indication of the changes that had taken place. For 350 years the armed forces had been the guarantee of white political power, and now they had transferred their loyalty to all the people of South Africa.

In his speech on the day of his inauguration, President Mandela said, 'Out of the experience of an extraordinary human disaster that lasted too long, must be born a society of which all humanity will be proud.' Much of the rest of what he said about South Africa can be applied to all parts of the world, including our own country. He thanked those who had come from other countries to join in South Africa's celebrations, and went on:

> *We trust that you will continue to stand by us as we tackle the challenges of building peace, prosperity, non-sexism, non-racialism and democracy.*
> *The time for healing of the wounds has come. The moment to bridge the chasms that divide us has come. The time to build is upon us.*

We have, at last, achieved our political emancipation. We pledge ourselves to liberate all our people from the continuing bondage of poverty, deprivation, suffering, gender and other discrimination.

We succeeded to take our last steps to freedom in conditions of relative peace. We commit ourselves to the construction of a complete, just and lasting peace.

We have triumphed in the effort to implant hope in the breasts of millions of our people. We enter into a covenant that we shall build the society in which all South Africans, both black and white, will be able to walk tall, without any fear in their hearts, assured of their unalienable right to human dignity – a rainbow nation at peace with itself and the world.

We understand that there is no easy road to freedom. We know that none of us acting alone can achieve success. We must, therefore, act together as a united people, for national reconciliation, for nation-building, for the birth of a new world.

Let there be justice for all. Let there be peace for all. Let there be work, bread, water and salt for all. Let each know that for each the body, the mind and the soul have been freed to fulfil themselves. Never, never and never again shall it be that this beautiful land will again experience the oppression of one by another and suffer the indignity of being the skunk of the world.

Let freedom reign. The sun shall never set on so glorious a human achievement. God bless Africa.

A spirit of hope and optimism was present in South Africa in May 1994. In the following March the Queen visited the country, now again a member of the Commonwealth. She had last been there forty-eight years earlier and had returned, as she said, 'to see for myself what is little short of a miracle'. Her arrival coincided with the thirty-fifth anniversary of the Sharpeville massacre, now commemorated as a public holiday; it has been called Human Rights Day to emphasize the importance of every human being. Too often we see how easily human nature can degenerate from what Nelson Mandela called 'the nobility of the human soul' into depravity and barbarity. Like him and the whole of South Africa, we must continually reassert our belief in justice and strengthen our confidence in the nobility of the human soul.

Ideals and Equality

A PRAYER

O God, we pray for peace and reconciliation throughout the world. May we receive inspiration from the transformation in South Africa, and strive for continued and steady progress to achieve a just society for all.

Amen.

Civilization and Mahatma Gandhi

✳ Gandhi as a spiritual leader and social reformer
✳ 'Civilization is the celebration of our differences.'
✳ Tolerance and acceptance of others
✳ Recognizing that our differences are our strengths
✳ Increasing contact for greater understanding
✳ The importance of what we have in common

The assembly refers to contact between young people of different countries and would be particularly appropriate when linked to exchange or other foreign visits.

A key sentence is repeated several times. Its effect might be enhanced if spoken by another voice.

Mahatma Gandhi was a political and spiritual leader in India and a social reformer of immense influence and authority. He was a Hindu and believed in non-violence. He played a major part in India's struggle to gain independence from Britain and was imprisoned by the British on many occasions. His methods of resistance were always passive and non-violent. He also campaigned for the most disadvantaged in India's society – the Untouchables. Although a Hindu, he attempted to unite Muslims and Hindus in India, but in the end, in 1948, soon after independence from Britain, he was assassinated by a Hindu extremist. He was a tiny man, but his stature as a great moral leader is enormous. He said many wise things including these words:

'Civilization is the celebration of our differences.'

When we are able to accept people for what they are, when we regard everyone as of equal worth whatever the colour of their skin, their sex, their intelligence, their language, their customs, their traditions, then indeed we can regard ourselves as a civilized people.

History is full of attempts to persecute or eliminate those who are different or seen as a threat. The extermination of over 6 million Jews by the Nazis is a constant reminder of the inhumanity and barbarity to which the human race can descend. In more recent years, the slaughtering of people in opposing tribes in Rwanda and the so-called 'ethnic cleansing' in Bosnia, Serbia and Croatia are further examples of uncivilized human behaviour, when other people are perceived as threatening. In too many places in the world, political opponents of dictators are imprisoned, tortured or killed, and mentally and physically handicapped people are put away out of sight.

But Gandhi said, 'Civilization is the celebration of our differences.'

In a school community, and in the wider community, we need to recognize that we are all different, but that we all have strengths and talents and that all our different strengths added together are formidable indeed. So, within our various communities, our differences are our strengths. Differences in background and religion bring a richness to life that should be cherished, and we need to guard carefully our freedom to express our opinions. We may be irritated at times by politicians and others who are quick to express their views and criticize those of others, particularly if we disagree with them, but it is very important that people have the freedom to argue different positions and to discuss matters openly. Of course, there are things that are wrong in our country, but we are able to express our views, criticize local and national government and other bodies, and put forward alternative ideas. Civilization is, indeed, the celebration of our differences.

Beyond our own country are millions of people with many differences from us, but all of them of equal worth. One of the enormous benefits of modern communications is the greater ease of contact that is possible between ordinary people who live in different parts of the world. This can occur through holidays and educational visits but in particular it is increasingly possible through exchanges and opportunities to welcome people from other countries into our own homes. There are now many opportunities to study abroad, both within the European Union and beyond. The more contact there is between people of different countries, the greater the understanding that develops; it soon becomes clear that the things that unite people are far more important than the things that divide them. Contacts between young people of different countries often begin at school and most schools, in a commitment to promoting international understanding, encourage links with other countries.

Within a school community or a local community, within our own country or throughout the world, there are many differences between us, but the recognition that the things that bring us together are more important than the things that divide us is a sign of civilization. Tolerance of others and valuing others whatever their strengths and weaknesses are important aspects of living in a civilized society. Remember Gandhi's words: 'Civilization is the celebration of our differences.'

A PRAYER

O God, help us to recognize that all of us have a contribution to make. Give us the gifts of tolerance and respect for others so that we can celebrate the individual worth of all people.

Amen.

Ideals and Equality

The United Nations of the World

✳ The origins of the U.N. and its strengths and weaknesses
✳ The U.N. Charter on human rights
✳ The Declaration of the Rights of the Child
✳ Importance of links and friendship between people
  throughout the world

This assembly would be particularly appropriate on or near
United Nations Day on 24th October. Posters about the work
of the U.N. could be displayed around the room.
    A number of pupils could be involved in the assembly,
with each in turn reading out sections of the Charter and the
Declaration.

In 1945 large areas of the world were in ruins, and few people
had been unaffected in one way or another by the horrors of
the Second World War. It had been the second catastrophic war to
afflict the world in thirty years, and it was as a result of this that the
United Nations Organization was formed. It is now more than fifty
years since its first meeting and, though there have been setbacks and
failures, the overwhelming majority of countries in the world belong to
it. The United Nations is an association of states pledged to maintain
international peace and security and to promote international co-operation.

The world of today is very different from the world of 1945, and the
United Nations of today is very different from the organization founded
over fifty years ago. Then it consisted of only a few countries; now, with
most countries in Africa and Asia having achieved independence, and
several other countries like the former Soviet Union having split into
separate parts, it is a huge organization of nearly 200 countries.

The United Nations has had its problems and we tend to hear more
about the failures than the successes. At times, its formal meetings
seem no more than propaganda for the more powerful countries; at

other times, it seems to be dominated by small countries who make a lot of noise but few positive contributions. Often it seems powerless to deal with major problems in the world, whether these are conflicts between or within countries, or human tragedies such as large-scale starvation in the poorest parts of the world.

On the other hand, many conflicts have been solved or at least helped by the intervention of the United Nations. Even in cases where the U.N.'s influence appears to have been limited, the consequences of non-intervention almost certainly would have been worse. Perhaps more important, most of the positive work of the United Nations is done outside the Security Council, the General Assembly and the peace-keeping missions; this work is carried out by various organizations sponsored by the U.N. such as the World Health Organization, the World Bank, the Food and Agriculture Organization, and the United Nations Children's Fund.

We need to be aware of the positive side of the United Nations and the value of co-operation throughout the world. Today, 24th October, is set aside throughout the world as a special day to think of the United Nations and its Charter which was agreed in 1945 to set out the aims of the organization. The Charter is a statement of what it believed in then and it still applies today. It sounds idealistic, but it is important to have ideals. If we don't have ideals, we have nothing to strive for. Here is the Charter of the United Nations in a summarized form.

WE THE PEOPLES OF THE UNITED NATIONS DETERMINED
To save succeeding generations from the scourge of war, and
To reaffirm faith in fundamental human rights and in the equal rights of men and women and of nations, large and small, and
To establish conditions under which justice and international law can be maintained, and
To promote social progress and better standards of life in larger freedom,
AND FOR THESE ENDS
To practise tolerance and live together in peace with one another as good neighbours, and
To unite our strength to maintain international peace and security, and

To ensure that armed force shall not be used, save in the common interest, and
To employ international machinery for the promotion of the economic and social advancement of the peoples,
HAVE RESOLVED TO COMBINE OUR EFFORTS TO ACCOMPLISH THESE AIMS
and do hereby establish an international organization to be known as
THE UNITED NATIONS

Human rights, including the rights of young people, have always been an important concern of the United Nations, and many years ago it published the United Nations Declaration of the Rights of the Child. Some of these rights may seem very obvious to us, but this should help us realize how much we now take for granted, while in some parts of the world these rights do not exist. Listen to the Declaration of the Rights of the Child that the United Nations has proclaimed.

The Right to affection, love and understanding.
The Right to adequate nutrition and medical care.
The Right to free education.
The Right to full opportunity for play and recreation.
The Right to a name and nationality.
The Right to special care, if handicapped.
The Right to be among the first to receive relief in times of disaster.
The Right to learn to be a useful member of society and to develop individual abilities.
The Right to be brought up in a spirit of peace and universal brotherhood.
The Right to enjoy these regardless of race, colour, sex, religion, national or social origin.

The United Nations Charter and the Declaration of the Rights of the Child are ideals to strive for. As individuals, we may wonder what we can do, but we should remember that the collective force of individuals to have an influence is very strong. One positive thing we can do is to take every opportunity to meet people from other parts of the world. Young people have a particular responsibility here and today have many opportunities for travel and to welcome others who come to this country to study or to take part in exchanges. The more we meet and get to know people from other countries, the stronger the understanding between the nations of the world will become and the more we shall realize how much we all have in common. We never think of fighting our friends: if friendship increasingly crosses international boundaries, the prospect of peace will be greater.

A PRAYER

O God, hear our prayer for all the people of the world. We remember especially those who suffer hunger, poverty or warfare. Strengthen the United Nations and all who work to bring peace and prosperity to the world. May we, who have so much, do all that we can to help others who have so little.

Amen.

Ideals and Equality

6

The Problem of Suffering

Natural Disasters

✳ Disasters – the example of the Lynmouth floods and the great storm of 1953
✳ The power of nature
✳ The mystery of suffering
✳ Finding inner strength and courage through suffering

Pictures and blown-up press cuttings about recent disasters could be displayed during the assembly or a newspaper extract read out.

We sometimes hear of disastrous floods, either in this country or abroad. In 1952, August was a particularly wet month in the West Country. Exmoor, in Somerset and north Devon, was saturated by the heavy rainfall of the previous few weeks, when, on 15th August, there was a violent cloudburst over the area drained by the East and West Lyn rivers. The rivers quickly became raging torrents, carrying huge boulders with them as vast amounts of water gushed down the valleys. The two rivers meet just before they reach the sea at the picturesque little settlement of Lynmouth. But that night terror and destruction reigned as floodwaters and huge rocks devastated the homes of many people in Lynmouth. On that dreadful night thirty-four people died and many of the houses in Lynmouth were destroyed.

The following winter, on 31st January 1953, there occurred during the day and night one of the worst storms ever to hit the British Isles. The first disaster happened in the morning. The ferry from Stranraer in Scotland set out for Larne in Northern Ireland. Only just over an hour of the journey is on the open sea – surely not long enough for things to go wrong? However, the ship was battered by huge seas and sank; of the 170 people on board, 132 were drowned.

As the storm moved east later that day and night, it struck the east coast of England and before the night was out, over 300 people were dead. The Lincolnshire coast was very badly affected. Between Mablethorpe and Sutton-on-Sea, the land was flooded by the sea for a kilometre inland from the coastline to a depth of over 3 metres. Further down the coast many houses were buried in sand up to the bedroom windows. At Hunstanton, in Norfolk, the 7.25 p.m. train had just left the station when it was hit by a bungalow that had been lifted off its foundations with two people still inside it. In Suffolk, the port of Felixstowe suffered badly. The southern part of the town, being on a peninsula between the North Sea and the estuary of the River Orwell, was almost engulfed: the sea burst in from one side and there was a great tidal surge from the other side. Forty-three people were killed.

In the years since 1952, the river beds in Lynmouth have been widened so that such disastrous floods don't happen again, and on the east coast much has been done since 1953 to strengthen the sea defences. But events such as the Lynmouth floods and the great storm of 1953 remind us of the awesome power of nature. They also make us think about one of the biggest mysteries of human life – the existence of suffering.

Why is there pain and suffering in the world? Why are innocent people killed in earthquakes and floods and other disasters?

One of the biggest stumbling blocks to religious belief is the problem of suffering. 'How can we believe in God,' people ask, 'when such terrible things happen?' 'If God exists, and he is good, loving and all powerful, why does he allow us to suffer?' There is no easy answer to this. It is impossible to attempt to assess the issues involved in just a short assembly, but a few thoughts might be helpful.

It is true to say that many people turn to God in times of trouble. When people are happy, they may forget about God; but when grief comes and sorrows overwhelm, then people are more likely to remember their God. It is often through suffering that people find a strength they didn't know they possessed; they become stronger as a

The Problem of Suffering

result and can very often inspire others. Doctors see this frequently. Here are some words written by one doctor about the courage and inspiration that can result from suffering.

> *On the whole it is true to say that suffering, courageously borne, lifts morale not only for the person but also for everyone else. I have seen patients in a ward who were undoubtedly among the most seriously afflicted by disease or injury, but whose courage was not only an example but a tremendous source of comfort to everyone else. And I have seen people go down to an operating theatre the braver because they had seen someone else go down the week before who set a good example. Courage, like fear, can be infectious. So showing courage in suffering can be a gift to the world. It is a gift which doctors are always glad to receive from their patients.*

(D. Stafford-Clark, *The Problem of Suffering*)

A comparison with plants in a garden is another way of illustrating the effects of suffering. When a plant is pruned, it suffers by losing many of its leaves and is cut back to only a small part of its former glory. But the plant most pruned by the gardener is the one which, when the following summer comes, will have the most beautiful blossoms and the most abundant fruit.

The problem of suffering is a difficult topic to deal with and one which has occupied the minds of people throughout history. It is useful to reflect on disasters like the Lynmouth floods and the great storm of 1953, and it is important to remember those who are suffering in any way and to try to help them in whatever way we can.

A PRAYER

O God, we pray for all whom we know to be suffering in any way at this time. We pray that they will not be destroyed by their suffering, but will find inner strength to come through it and to grow in spirit because of it.

Amen.

Learning from Suffering

* Causes of suffering
* Creativity despite mental or physical suffering
* Development of character through facing adversity
* Buchenwald Concentration Camp – the effects of suffering
* Taking opportunities and rising to challenges

The assembly could end with a short period of reflection about the theme, during which a recording of part of the last movement of Beethoven's Ninth Symphony (the 'Choral') could be played. This supreme achievement epitomizes triumph over adversity.

Reports of floods, storms, earthquakes or other disasters that cause death and injury, often make us think about the problems of suffering. We might ask why, if there is a good, all-loving and powerful God, suffering should occur. 'Why does he allow it to happen?' There are, of course, no easy answers to this fundamental question, and many people spend much of their lives searching for answers to this and similar questions. The search, however, enables us to explore our own thoughts and ideas, and, as a result, we may learn more about human nature and the world in which we live.

Sometimes suffering can be useful. An aching tooth tells us that our teeth need attention, and the pain from scalding water tells us very clearly to be careful! Much pain and suffering arise from people's selfishness and wrong choices and misuse of the freedom that God has given. Can we blame God for this?

There are those who suffer for causes they believe in. Many religious and political leaders, such as Mahatma Gandhi and Martin Luther King, have died for their causes. For Christians, the supreme example is Jesus Christ who, they believe, died a cruel death on the cross in order to save the world from its sins.

The Problem of Suffering

Many great works of art have been created by people who have suffered, either physically or mentally. Beethoven composed some of his greatest works after he became deaf. Van Gogh, though in mental turmoil, was able to produce magnificent paintings. These examples show that through suffering can come creativity.

Very often suffering brings people together. In times of war or natural disasters, the bond between people strengthens as they face difficulties together. Undoubtedly, suffering is a challenge that has to be met. Many people find an inner strength in suffering and become better people because of it.

Buchenwald Concentration Camp, like all concentration camps of the Second World War, was the scene of immense suffering. A Frenchman who had been imprisoned there for two years wrote about the camp and the effects it had on different people. He analysed the character of some of the men and the effect that the suffering had on them. There were only men in this camp, but what he says, of course, applies equally to men and women.

Under the stresses and strains imposed by life in the camp, only one thing prevailed – strength of character. Cleverness, creativeness, learning, all went down; only real goodness survived.

Sooner or later weakness of fibre was revealed in a man, and sooner or later it destroyed him. Self-discipline was essential, and this was the basis of character. For instance – the question of the open fire. It had been very tempting, especially in the cold winter nights, to go and lie by the open braziers in our blockhouse. But it was fatal. A man began by lying some distance from the fire, on the outer ring. But the fire drew like a magnet. He would go closer to the flames, until finally he would get as near as he possibly could. The contrast between the heat of the fire at night and the cold of the roll-call in the morning was too much for these poor human frames. It was only a matter of time before it killed them.

The fact that every prisoner knew this did not prevent a great number from succumbing. If a prisoner began habitually to leave his bunk in the night and lie down to sleep on the floor around the fire, you knew that he had decided, even if he had not faced his own decision, that death was preferable to discomfort.

It seemed to me that those men displayed most character who had the capacity for living on their own and that these men possessed something that is easiest to describe as religion, faith or devotion. I saw that leadership exercised by Christians. I saw it in communists, too. It was displayed by people who had no religious faith or political creed in any formal sense, but who still had some inner core which gave them a belief in life, when the rest of us were lost.

The camp showed me that a man's real enemies are not ranged against him along the borders of a hostile country; they are often among his own people – indeed, within his own mind. The worst enemies are hate and greed, and cruelty. The real enemy is within.

(Pierre d'Harcourt, *The Real Enemy*, slightly adapted)

It's an interesting commentary on human character. It would be wrong to suggest that it's a good thing to suffer just so that we can develop our character. However, it is true to say that we should try to learn from our suffering so that something is gained from it. We need to take every opportunity to develop our strengths and to rise to challenges – in our work, in sport, in music, in hobbies, in everything we do. The more we do to develop our characters in every direction, the better we shall be able to cope with problems when they arise, and the better we shall be able to help others in their times of difficulty.

A PRAYER

O God, when we suffer, may we be tested and strengthened by it. May it leave us more reflective, with deepened emotions and heightened sensitivity to others. May we come through our suffering as better individuals.

Amen.

Remembering War

✳ Remembering the tragedy of war
✳ The dangers of glorifying war, but also the dangers of forgetting the horrors of war
✳ How should we remember war?
✳ The place of remembrance in efforts to strive for peace

Different schools will have different traditions for acts of remembrance, and many will use hymns and music associated with these events. This assembly can be adapted as required to fit into the tradition of your school. Music from Holst's 'Planets' Suite' could be used very effectively. 'Mars, the Bringer of War' was composed just before the outbreak of the First World War; Holst had never heard a machine-gun, but the music was surely prophetic of the terrors and brutality of mechanized warfare. 'Venus, the Bringer of Peace' is a complete and beautiful contrast to 'Mars', suggesting calmness and serenity. Used together they can illustrate the horrors of war and the necessity for peace.

As the fiftieth anniversary of the end of the Second World War becomes more distant, teachers may wish to adapt or update the remarks in the opening paragraph.

June 1994 marked the fiftieth anniversary of the D-Day landings on the beaches of Normandy in northern France. This was the beginning of the events which eventually led to the end of the Second World War and to the tyranny of the Nazis in Europe. Great celebrations took place on 8th May 1995 on the fiftieth anniversary of V.E. Day – Victory in Europe Day – though, as everyone knows, the war continued in the Far East for several more months during which time two atomic bombs were dropped on the Japanese cities of Hiroshima and Nagasaki. The war did not end completely until V.J. Day – Victory over Japan Day – in August 1945.

Early November is a time when we particularly think about the tragedy of war and remember those who have been killed or wounded in war. It was on 11th November 1918 that the First World War came to an end. For many years afterwards, Armistice Day, as it was called, was observed on 11th November. We now know it as Remembrance Day and it is always held on the second Sunday in November. Remembrance is very important because it reminds us of the tragedy of war.

Of course, there are dangers in remembering war; the uniforms, the medals, the parades, the display of arms and the patriotic tunes can all lead to the glorifying of war. But there are also dangers – for those of us who have not experienced war – of forgetting. There is the danger of forgetting the horror and suffering of war, of forgetting the millions of young soldiers who died prematurely, of forgetting the wholesale destruction of all that people had lovingly built up, and the danger of forgetting the cost, the waste, the loss, the fear and the pain. Many people still live with the scars of war, both physical and mental.

But how should we remember war? For thousands of former soldiers, the parades on Remembrance Sunday are of great importance. It is a time for them to remember the battles they fought and to grieve collectively for those of their comrades who died. It is also an opportunity for them to receive from us our respect for their achievements and our thanks for what they may have suffered in lost health on our behalf. For thousands of others, the grief is a private grief. For them, the parades are not appropriate; theirs is a quiet, private remembering of the part they played in war.

In some places, the ceremonies of remembrance are very simple but very moving. In the town of Ypres in northern France, a simple ceremony has been performed every night since the early 1920s. At 8 p.m. beneath the Menin Gate, built as a memorial arch to the thousands of soldiers who died in the area during the First World War but have no known grave, members of the local fire brigade perform the Last Post. There is no elaborate ceremony, no army bands and no marching soldiers, just the haunting bugle notes that echo poignantly in the night.

The war cemeteries in northern France, with their thousands and thousands of gravestones of those killed in both world wars, are a moving reminder of the reality of war. Britain too has several war cemeteries. Just outside Cambridge, for example, is an American war

The Problem of Suffering

The Problem of Suffering

cemetery where thousands of Americans killed in Europe in the Second World War are buried, and in Newark's cemetery are the graves of hundreds of Polish soldiers whose bodies were brought there after they had been killed in war.

There are other reminders of war all around. In this country, the central parts of some of our ancient cities were virtually destroyed by enemy action. The centres of Coventry, Plymouth and Hull, for example, were completely rebuilt after the Second World War.

The same happened in Germany. Towns at strategic crossing points on the River Rhine were destroyed by British and American troops and aircraft as the Allies approached the Ruhr industrial area. In other parts of Germany, cities such as Dresden suffered wholesale destruction in the later stages of the war. No one who has seen photographs of Hiroshima after the first atomic bomb had been dropped can doubt the devastation that war can bring.

Remembering, then, is one way of thinking about the horrors of war. All wars are evil. The question is: which is the greater evil – war itself or the evil that war is trying to eliminate? Remembrance Sunday reminds us of the tragedy of war. It should also help us to strive continually for peace and to eliminate from the world the evils which lead to war. If we can do that, the world will be a better place and those who have died and suffered will not have done so in vain.

Wilfred Owen was a soldier in the First World War. He was killed just before the war ended in 1918. He was twenty-five years old when he died, and he shared the fate of millions of other young people on both sides. Here is part of one of his poems, subtitled 'On seeing a piece of our artillery brought into action':

> *Be slowly lifted up, thou long black arm,*
> *Great gun towering towards Heaven, about to curse; ...*
>
> *Reach at that arrogance which needs thy harm,*
> *And beat it down before its sins grow worse; ...*
>
> *But when thy spell be cast complete and whole,*
> *May God curse thee, and cut thee from our soul!*

The following words are often spoken at services of remembrance for those killed in war. They are a reminder particularly that, in war, it is usually the young who are killed on the battlefields. Away from the fields of battle it is invariably the innocent who suffer.

They shall not grow old as we that are left grow old.
Age shall not weary them, nor the years condemn.
At the going down of the sun, and in the morning,
We shall remember them.

A PRAYER

O God, we give thanks for all the blessings which are ours today. We remember and give thanks for all the people in the past who have fought to give us the freedom we now enjoy. We pray for those who still suffer because of war and for those who have bitter memories. We ask that the time will come when all people will learn to live in peace and share the good things of this earth, so that the world may be a happier place.

Amen.

The Problem of Suffering

Death of a Member of the School Community

✳ Some thoughts, readings and prayers that may be helpful to those leading assemblies in these circumstances

The death of a pupil or an adult within the school community is deeply sad and traumatic. It is a time when the quality of leadership and example is crucial; the sensitivity with which that leadership is displayed will be of great help and comfort in the difficult days that follow. The circumstances of each case will be unique, depending on the age of the person, the cause of death, whether it was sudden and unexpected or following a long illness, the personality of the pupil or adult, whether there are brothers and sisters, and many other factors. It would be quite inappropriate to suggest a suitable assembly following a death since the assembly must be prepared very carefully to meet, as far as possible, the particular circumstances. What I have done is to bring together a number of readings, quotations and thoughts that I have found helpful on such occasions. Obviously what is appropriate for a particular occasion will be a matter of individual judgement. I hope such occasions are rare indeed.

None of us can pretend to understand why a young life should end so prematurely and tragically. It seems such a waste – all young people have so much to give. We are bound to question it and to wonder what life is all about and why we are here. We need time to grieve, and not to be ashamed of grieving. We need to comfort family and friends. None of these questions is easy to answer. None of these emotions is easy to handle.

We all will die sometime – death is the only certainty there is. It is part of the pattern of the universe and creation. When we die will vary and depends on many things. Today, in this country, relatively few children die. That was not the case in the past, nor is it so in some parts of the world now. But it is still very difficult to understand why it should happen to someone who could expect to look forward to so much on this earth; it is one of the great mysteries of life itself. Although we must not be morbid about death, it is right and natural to be sad and to think about those in the family and close friends who mourn the loss of a dear one.

In death we need to try to see the positive, for, unless we do, life itself has little meaning. The qualities shown in the life that has ended can surely provide inspiration for our own lives. Our life on earth is like the bud of a flower; the memory is the flower coming into full bloom. At a time of death, the qualities of true friendship are very important to those who need help and support.

St Paul said, 'We are no better than pots of earthenware to contain this treasure' (2 Corinthians 4:7). An earthenware pot can be broken easily, but the treasure that is in the pot is not broken. In death, the body is broken, but the treasure that is in the body is unbreakable and lasts for ever.

Death is nothing at all. I have only slipped away into the next room. I am I, and you are you. Whatever we were to each other, that we still are. Call me by my old familiar name, speak to me in the easy way which you always used. Put no difference in your tone, wear no forced air of solemnity or sorrow. Laugh as we always laughed at the little jokes we enjoyed together. Let my name be ever the household word that it always was, let it be spoken without effort, without the trace of shadow on it. Life means all that it ever meant. It is the same as it ever was; there is unbroken continuity. Why should I be out of mind because I am out of sight? I am waiting for you, for an interval, somewhere very near, just round the corner. All is well.

(Henry Holland, 1847–1918, Canon of St Paul's Cathedral)

I don't know whether I believe in a future life, but I believe that all that you go through here must have some value, therefore there must be some reason. And there must be some 'going on'. How exactly that happens I've never been able to decide. There is a future – that I'm sure of. But how, that I don't know. And I came to feel that it didn't really matter very much because whatever the future held you'd have to face it when you came to it, just as whatever life holds you have to face it in exactly the same way. And the important thing was that you never let down doing the best that you were able to do – it might be poor because you might not have much within you to give, or to help other people with, or to live your life with. But as long as you did the very best thing that you were able to do, then that was what you were put here to do and that was what you were accomplishing by being here.

(Eleanor Roosevelt, *This I Believe*)

On his arrival, Jesus found that Lazarus had already been in the tomb for four days. Bethany was less than two miles from Jerusalem, and many Jews had come to Martha and Mary to comfort them in the loss of their brother. When Martha heard that Jesus was coming, she went out to meet him, but Mary stayed at home.
'Lord,' Martha said to Jesus, 'if you had been here, my brother would not have died. But I know that even now God will give you whatever you ask.'
Jesus said to her, 'Your brother will rise again.'
Martha answered, 'I know he will rise again in the resurrection at the last day.'
Jesus said to her, 'I am the resurrection and the life. He who believes in me will live, even though he dies; and whoever lives and believes in me will never die. Do you believe this?'
'Yes, Lord,' she told him, 'I believe that you are the Christ, the Son of God, who was to come into the world.'

(John 11:17–27)

Make us channels of your peace;
Where there is hatred, let us bring love;
Where there is injury, let us bring pardon;
Where there is doubt, true faith in you;
Where there is despair in life, let us bring hope;

Where there is darkness, only light;
Where there is sadness, ever joy. Amen.

(St Francis of Assisi)

SOME PRAYERS

✦

O God, comfort all who mourn for the loss of those dear to them. Be with them in their sorrow. Give them faith to look beyond the troubles of the present time, and to know that neither life nor death can separate us from your love.

Amen.

O God, we pray for those whom we know and love but see no longer. Grant them your peace; let perpetual light shine upon them. In your loving wisdom and almighty power, work in them your good purpose.

Amen.

O God, help us to trust in you when things occur that we neither welcome nor understand. Give us the sensitivity to feel for the sorrows of others. Strengthen all who mourn and comfort those who are bereaved.

Amen.

7

Traditions and Cultural Diversity

Customs and Traditions

* The Hindu festival of Divali
* Celtic New Year, Hallowe'en and All Saints' Day
* Guy Fawkes' Day
* Adaptation of pagan festivals by the Church
* Intolerance and persecution
* Celebration of cultural diversity

If possible, some representatives of the local Hindu community (pupils or others) could be present, in traditional dress, and perhaps talk about the traditions associated with Divali. A number of pupils could also dress up in Hallowe'en and Guy Fawkes images and recite the rhyme quoted below. The leader's role would be to link the different customs and traditions together.

The period of late October and early November is a time of the year when several traditional customs and religious festivals occur. The great Hindu festival of Divali takes place at this time of year, sometimes in October and sometimes in November, the exact date depending on the phases of the moon. On 31st October there is Hallowe'en, followed on 1st November by All Saints' or All Hallows' Day. On 5th November a different custom is celebrated – Guy Fawkes' Day or Bonfire Night.

The name Hallowe'en is a shortened version of 'the evening before All Hallows' Day'. Originally the pagan festival of Samain – summer's end – was celebrated at this season. In pre-Christian times the Celtic New Year began on 1st November and Samain was the pagan fire festival that marked the end of summer. On this night the dead were believed to return to their old homes to warm themselves in front of the fire. It was also the witches' festival and the masks and turnip lanterns of today are a reminder of witches and ghosts of old. As with several other traditional festivals, the Christian Church turned Samain and the Celtic New Year into a special festival of remembrance, offering prayers for all the saints on 1st November (All Saints' or All Hallows' Day) and remembering the rest of the dead on 2nd November (All Souls' Day).

But pagan ideas remained, mixed in with the beliefs of Christianity. It was thought that evil spirits made the most of Hallowe'en because they would not dare go about on All Saints' Day. So it became the custom on Hallowe'en to beware not only of spirits and ghosts, but of witches and all sorts of other strange powers. This was combined with the earlier practice of the fire festival of Samain, and great bonfires were lit on hilltops as people sought to drive away all evil forces from the land.

The lighting of bonfires on 5th November has links with this tradition. Everyone knows of the plot in 1605 of a group of Roman Catholics, who were being persecuted at that time, to blow up the King, Lords and Commons in Parliament. Guy Fawkes was ready in the cellar with his lantern and a slow match, but he was discovered and, with the other conspirators, put to death. The Puritans were not happy about mixing pagan customs and Christian worship, so when Parliament ordered a public holiday to celebrate the failure of the Gunpowder Plot, it was seized upon as a replacement for Hallowe'en as a festival day. For about 250 years, 5th November was a public holiday but, unfortunately, it became a day when hatred was stirred up against Roman Catholics. An effigy of the Pope was sometimes burnt as well as the effigy of Guy Fawkes. Most people know the rhyme:

Remember, remember the fifth of November,
Gunpowder, treason and plot.
I see no reason why gunpowder treason,
Should ever be forgot.

Traditions and Cultural Diversity

125

But for many years a second verse was also commonly repeated:

A rope, a rope to hang the Pope,
A piece of cheese to toast him;
A barrel of beer to drink his health,
And a right good fire to roast him.

This persecution and stirring up of hatred shows the worst sort of religious intolerance. Some traditions also, like Hallowe'en, can place too much emphasis on evil and fear. The days of hostility between people based on religious belief should be long past but, unhappily, we still see examples of hatred and intolerance. Instead, we should enjoy sharing the celebrations, festivals and traditions of all groups of people. It is a happy coincidence that Hindus celebrate one of their most important festivals with fireworks at much the same time of year that many of us are letting off fireworks and lighting bonfires in commemoration of a distant historical event.

Divali is a festival of lights. The name comes from a Sanskrit word meaning 'a row of lights'. Hindus in Britain celebrate by exchanging presents and holding parties; fireworks are set off, homes are decorated and, in some areas, whole streets are lit up. In Leicester, for example, the Belgrave Road area of the city is a dazzling sight at Divali. It is a colourful place at any time, with shops selling beautiful saris and many other things from various cultural backgrounds. At Divali it is even more striking: the road is lit up with decorations and signs saying 'Happy Divali' and 'A Happy New Year'. On Divali night itself there are spectacular firework displays.

For Hindus, Divali is a time of rejoicing, with lights, fireworks and the exchange of gifts. It is a time of thanksgiving for the previous year and a time to ask for blessing in the year that lies ahead. Houses and temples are filled with lights and lamps, and people wear new clothes and visit friends, as well as exchanging gifts.

Sikhs share the Divali festival of lights with Hindus but celebrate for totally different reasons. (The Sikh festival celebrates the release from over twelve months' imprisonment of the Sixth Guru, Har Gobind, and has no connection with the story of the Hindu deities Rama and Sita.)

All of us, whatever our religion or beliefs, can rejoice with Hindus and Sikhs at Divali. Their celebrations remind us of what we have in common. Divali is a festival of light, just as Christmas is for Christians. An important symbol of Christmas is the Star of Bethlehem – the light that brought people to Jesus. In the darker days of winter, these festivals of light help to strengthen our faith. When we enjoy the fun of fireworks and bonfires, instead of remembering the divisions that religion has caused, let us celebrate the things that unite us and all the hopes and ideals we have in common. Let us celebrate the richness that religion brings to people's lives.

A HINDU PRAYER

May all be happy. May all be free from suffering. May all see what is good. May the good attain peace. May the peaceful be free from bondage. May the free make others free.

Amen.

Israel and the Jewish New Year

* The traditions and significance of the New Year and the Day of Atonement
* The problems of Palestine
* Persecution of Jews and displacement of Palestinians
* The Ten Commandments and the similarities of other moral codes

On or around the Jewish New Year in September is the obvious time for this assembly, but it would also be appropriate whenever events in the Middle East are topical. A large map of the area would be a useful visual aid. ('Hashanah' is pronounced with the stress on the second syllable.)

Traditions and Cultural Diversity

127

In Britain, September is the traditional time for the new school year to start. But for many people throughout the world September marks the beginning of their new year. These people use the traditional greeting 'Shanah tovah' on their New Year's Day. It means 'a good new year' and it is the customary greeting of Jewish people everywhere. In this country, years are numbered from the date of the birth of Christ about 2000 years ago. Jews number their years from the time when Jewish tradition believed that the world was created. The Jewish number for the year 1990 is 5751; so 1995 is 5756, 2000 is 5761 and so on. The Jewish calendar, like many others, is based on the moon, so the exact day for the beginning of the New Year varies from year to year. Of course most modern Jews don't believe the world was literally created about 5800 years ago, but they still follow the traditional numbering.

The festival of the Jewish New Year is called Rosh Hashanah. It is a solemn time, when Jews think about what they have done wrong in the past year and make promises to themselves and to God to do better in the future. The period ends after ten days with the Jews' most holy day – Yom Kippur, the Day of Atonement.

Jews live in countries all over the world. It is only since 1948 that they have had a country they could call their own. That country is the state of Israel in the part of the world generally known as the Middle East; it is called Israel because one of the former names of the Jewish people was the 'Israelites'. Although only about fifty years old, the state of Israel has had a turbulent history as a result of conflict with its neighbouring countries. The problems are very considerable and it will be many years before all the issues are resolved, but a significant, if small, step towards a lasting peace was taken in September 1993, just before the beginning of the Jewish year 5754.

In September 1993, the Government of Israel and the leaders of the Palestinian people signed an agreement which is intended to pave the way towards a permanent settlement of the troubles of this area. Throughout a long and complex history, different groups of people, including Jews, Christians and Muslims, have fought for the land they believe is theirs. At the heart of the problem have been the conflicting interests of the Jewish and Palestinian people. When the state of Israel was created, there was violent bloodshed. Since then, as well as more or less continuous violence and terrorism, there have been several major wars, including one that is usually known as the Yom Kippur War. It was on this most holy of Jewish days that the state of Israel was attacked by some of its enemies. The attack was followed by massive retaliation by the Israelis.

One of the best-known stories in the Bible tells how David killed the giant Goliath, some 3000 years ago. David was an Israelite, Goliath a Philistine. From the name 'Israelite', we get Israel; from the word 'Philistine', we get Palestine. You could, therefore, with much truth, say that 3000 years ago the Israelis and the Palestinians were already in conflict over the same piece of land.

For much of the 3000 years since then, the Jews have been scattered over the world and have suffered a great deal of persecution, including the atrocities of the Nazis before and during the Second World War. The extermination of over 6 million Jews in concentration camps and elsewhere revealed the barbarity of human behaviour in the worst possible way. It was after the Second World War that the modern Jewish state of Israel was created in the area that Jews have always thought of as the 'Promised Land'. But the problem has been that the creation of Israel has meant the displacement of millions of Palestinians who have also regarded the area as their rightful land.

Everyone must hope that, in due course, Jews and Palestinians will be able to live in peace, and that the land between the Mediterranean Sea and the River Jordan will live up to its biblical description as a land 'flowing with milk and honey'. The Jewish New Year is an appropriate time to reflect on this historic but troubled part of the world where people of many different traditions find themselves together. Despite our differences, it is important to recognize all the things we have in common. The Ten Commandments, given by God to Moses in this place that is now so troubled, form the basis of the moral code of several of the world's great religions, and we are reminded again that the things that unite people are much more important than the things that divide them. The Ten Commandments were originally part of the law of the Israelites, but most religions and codes of living are based on similar principles.

Here is an abbreviated version of the Commandments.

You shall have no other gods except me.
You shall not make any idol for yourself.

You shall not misuse the name of God.
Remember to keep the sabbath day holy.
Honour your father and your mother.
You shall not commit murder.
You shall not commit adultery.
You shall not steal.
You shall not give false evidence.
You shall not covet things that are not yours.

(Adapted from Exodus 20:3–17)

A PRAYER

❂

O God, we pray for peace throughout the world and, especially today, for peace in the Middle East. We pray for all the people of this area – Jews, Muslims, Christians and others – that they may all have the opportunity to live in peace, sharing those things that unite them.

Amen.

Chinese New Year

❋ Celebration of cultural diversity
❋ Chinese communities and their traditions
❋ Animals of the Chinese years
❋ Is there anything in astrology?
❋ The importance of the individual

This assembly is most appropriate at the period of the Chinese New Year in late January or early February. It could be linked with displays of Chinese art and culture; you may be able to borrow such things as menus, crockery and chop-sticks from a local Chinese restaurant. If pupils are studying the festival as part of their classwork they could make masks or costumes to represent the twelve animals of the Chinese calendar and a procession could be held, with appropriate music.

Some extracts from a current horoscope will be needed for the reading.

The population of China is greater than that of any other country in the world; in fact, about a quarter of the world's population lives in China. The Chinese celebrate the beginning of their new year in late January or February. There are many Chinese people living in Britain and in some of our larger cities there are particular districts where Chinese restaurants, supermarkets and shops can be found, as well as other examples of Chinese culture. In virtually every British town there are Chinese restaurants, many of which put on special menus and functions to celebrate the Chinese New Year. By sharing with the Chinese community their own particular festival, we can help to celebrate the cultural diversity of our world.

Yuan Tan – New Year's Day – is a very colourful festival, celebrated with fireworks, dances and the giving of gifts, flowers and sweets. One distinctive feature is the famous lion dance, and firecrackers are let off

Traditions and Cultural Diversity

to frighten away evil spirits. Indeed, it was the Chinese who first invented fireworks. The whole New Year period lasts for a fortnight.

Most people know that the Chinese dedicate each year to one of twelve animals. These are the Rat, the Ox, the Tiger, the Rabbit (or Hare), the Dragon, the Snake, the Horse, the Sheep, the Monkey, the Cockerel, the Dog and the Pig. The years are always in this order. There is a legend that the animals were arguing about the name of the next year; each thought it should have its own name. So they decided on a race across a river. The Ox was in the lead, but the Rat had jumped on to the Ox's back, and at the far bank the Rat jumped off and landed first! The others finished in the order we have just heard.

The Chinese people believe that we inherit the characteristics of the animal of the year of our birth. What year were you born in? Have you got the characteristics of that animal? Let's start the sequence in 1978 – that was the year of the Horse; if you were born in 1979, you were born in the year of the Sheep. 1980 was the year of the Monkey,1981 the Cockerel, 1982 the Dog, 1983 the Pig. 1984 marked the beginning of the cycle as the year of the Rat; 1985 was the Ox, 1986 the Tiger, 1987 the Rabbit (or Hare), 1988 the Dragon, 1989 the Snake, and 1990 was back to the Horse. You can easily work out the present sequence, with the cycle starting again with the Rat in 1996.

What are the characteristics of each of these animals? We will all have our own opinions about them, and will, no doubt, disagree particularly about the animal of the year of our birth. A Dog – faithful? Affectionate? Noisy? A Snake – clever? Untrustworthy? A Pig – probably a much maligned animal which is really very clean. Is it steady and persistent? The idea of inheriting characteristics at birth is an interesting one. Many people believe in birth signs. The study of these signs is known as astrology, and no popular paper or magazine would be complete without its horoscope. It is interesting that the number twelve frequently occurs in astrology just as it does in most calendar systems. There are twelve signs of the zodiac, some of them also named after animals – Taurus the bull, Cancer the crab, Leo the lion, Pisces the fish. Some people take their stars very seriously, while others treat them as a bit of fun or regard them as nonsense. Here are one or two extracts from a recent horoscope.

(At this point the leader can read a few extracts from an appropriate horoscope, possibly their own 'stars' for the day.)

Is this just a lot of relatively harmless nonsense, or is there something in it? Are the Chinese right in believing that the year of your birth, and even the time of day, is significant? Whatever you believe, the marvellous thing is that we are all different. There is no one else in the world quite like any one of us. We are all unique individuals. Many would say that this individuality is given by God, that it is not chance, not the stars, not the animal of a particular year that gives us our unique individuality, but our Creator. Different religions and traditions have their own particular beliefs, but most emphasize the importance of the individual within the order established by a supreme Creator.

A PRAYER

O God, we are thankful for the lessons we can learn from other people throughout the world. Above all, we marvel at human life and the miracle of our uniqueness as individuals.

Amen.

Richness and Diversity of Culture

✳ Muslim influence in southern Spain
✳ Muslim and Christian architecture in harmony
✳ Tolerance and intolerance
✳ Richness of diversity

A large map of Spain highlighting key areas and holiday destinations could be displayed and posters of Granada and Córdoba might be available from the Spanish Tourist Board. A recording of some traditional Andalucian music would help to set the scene. Falla's 'Nights in the Gardens of Spain' was inspired by Andalucian folk music and the gardens depicted include the Generalife Gardens within the Alhambra in Granada.

Traditions and Cultural Diversity

T he south of Spain is a very popular destination for holidays; this area is usually known as the Costa del Sol, and many people from Britain and other parts of Northern Europe go there, to places like Torremolinos and Marbella, to enjoy the sun and the sea. The area is also a popular location for film sets.

However, there is much more to the south of Spain than the Costa del Sol, some of it of great historical and architectural interest. The south of Spain is quite different from the rest of Spain, and it is still usually known by its traditional name of Andalucia. One of the reasons why it is very different is that, for several hundred years, Andalucia was part of the Muslim world, following the religion of Islam. The Muslim influence on southern Spain is still most noticeable.

There are several fine cities where the Muslim influence is much in evidence. Two of them – Granada and Córdoba – contain two of the most wonderful buildings of the world. In Granada, the Alhambra stands on a hill dominating the city. It is really a large complex of buildings – part fortress, part palace, and partly the setting of extraordinarily beautiful gardens. At the heart of the Alhambra are a series of palaces, each with courtyards of great beauty. These were built for the Arab princes and princesses who ruled the area. The rich carvings of the walls are exquisite; the design, the decorations and the use of water bring a peace and restfulness that contrast with the heat of a Spanish summer.

In Córdoba, there is one of the largest and most extraordinary buildings in the world. The Muslims started building their Mosque in Córdoba in the year 785 – over 1200 years ago. Again, the building contains some extremely beautiful stone carvings, but the predominant memory of the building is of hundreds and hundreds of columns and round arches radiating out in all directions. In 1236, Córdoba was conquered by Christian forces and the Muslims overthrown. Then began the process in which the building became a Christian place of worship rather than a Muslim one. For nearly 300 years only minor changes were made to the building, but in the sixteenth century the central part of the Mosque was pulled down and a Cathedral built within it.

The result today is a building that is almost unbelievable. You can wander for some time amongst the columns of the original Mosque, and then suddenly, within the Mosque, you come across a large Cathedral. It is also of great beauty, but in a totally different style from the Arab Mosque. There was a good deal of controversy when the

Cathedral was first built inside the Mosque, but today most agree that the two essential parts of the whole and their two great influences – Muslim and Christian – exist in perfect harmony side by side.

Andalucia is a graphic example of the immense influence that different cultures can have on an area. The combination of Muslim, Christian and other influences brings a great richness to the beauty and culture of the area. Indeed, within a very short distance of the Mosque in Córdoba is the Roman Bridge across the River Guadalquivir and the fascinating old Jewish quarter. The period following the Christian reconquest of southern Spain was a time of great intolerance which led to the expulsion of the Arabs and Jews from Spain. But, if you look at southern Spain today, it is the combination of all the different influences that gives the area its vitality, its distinctiveness and much of its interest.

We can extend this idea to our own lives. We are all different, but between us this diversity brings a tremendous richness to life from which we can all benefit. To benefit from this diversity, though, we need to show tolerance towards each other. If we don't accept the qualities that others can bring, life as a whole will be the poorer. It is a tragedy that, in some areas – such as the former Yugoslavia – where the diversity of people should be a strength, conflicts arise between different ethnic groups and traditions. We need to ensure that, in the school community and in the wider community, we are never intolerant towards different, but equally worthy, individuals and groups.

If you ever have the opportunity to go to southern Spain, try to visit the Alhambra in Granada and the Mosque in Córdoba. They demonstrate how different cultures, styles and influences can exist side by side in harmony and as part of a unified whole.

A PRAYER

O God, we ask for the gift of tolerance. We pray that we may learn to value the qualities of other people so that we can work together for the benefit of all.

Amen.

Traditions and Cultural Diversity

May Day and Spring

* Ancient origins of May Day celebrations
* Traditions associated with May Day and the coming of spring
* International labour movement and May Day parades
* Optimism of spring and reawakening of life

Early May is the obvious time for this assembly. There are various opportunities for music within the assembly: a recording of some Morris dancing music could be played; a madrigal could be played or sung by a choir; other music associated with spring and the awakening of life could be used as an introduction or a conclusion — for example, 'Spring' from Vivaldi's 'Four Seasons' or 'Morning' from Grieg's 'Peer Gynt' suite.

The newest public holiday in Britain is the May Day holiday on the first Monday in May. Some people think that the holiday and celebrations should always be on the first day of May itself, whatever day of the week that happens to be. Indeed, in many other European countries there has been a public holiday on 1st May for many years. May Day celebrations themselves go back to ancient times.

In pre-Christian times, May was the time when spring was celebrated. In ancient Rome, young people spent the early part of May in the fields, singing and dancing in honour of Flora, the goddess of fruit and flowers, and gathering flowers for her temple. When the Romans conquered Britain and other countries, they brought this custom with them. After they left, although Christianity had become the main religion, spring was still celebrated with flowers.

So, by the Middle Ages, Christians in Britain were marking the changes in seasons, but, as so often happens, additional customs were borrowed from other cultures. Morris dances became part of the celebrations. These were introduced from Spain during the reign of Edward III. Some of the people in Spain at that time were called Moors, or Moriscos, and our Morris dances are adaptations of the military dances of the Moriscos. A key character in the dances was a boy wearing a headpiece known as a 'morione'. He was called the Mad Morion. A change of sex and a slight change in name gives us Maid Marion, who features with Robin Hood in some of the dances to this day. Another feature that has become part of the tradition is the singing of madrigals from the tower of Magdalen College in Oxford at six o'clock in the morning on the first day of May.

The maypole became the centre of celebrations in many villages and towns. This was a tall pole set upright and colourfully decorated with wreaths of flowers and ribbons. After this the young girl chosen as the May Queen was crowned. The rest of the day was spent dancing around the maypole, eating, drinking and having a good time. In some villages many of these customs continue, particularly the tradition of children dancing around the maypole. In the Nottinghamshire village of Wellow, a large permanent maypole still stands prominently in the middle of the village green.

Much more recently, May Day has been associated with the international labour movement. For many years, pictures of the May Day parade in Moscow dominated reporting of May Day celebrations. The day has always been an important one for the Trades Union movement. It was in 1890 that leaders of labour movements in Europe and America joined together to organize demonstrations pressing for a statutory eight-hour working day. These demonstrations were planned for the beginning of May, and on 4th May 1890, over 200,000 people crowded into Hyde Park in London to show their support for the cause. Engels, a friend of Karl Marx, wrote of 'the awakening of the working class from its winter sleep'. This sort of celebration is rather different from the rituals of welcoming the spring with flowers and dancing. Today, people take the opportunity of the public holiday to join in the many types of events that are organized all over the country.

So, at the beginning of May, people have celebrated for thousands of years the awakening of the earth in spring and their hopes for the future. This poem, 'The Spring' by Peter Howard, attempts to capture the optimism of spring and the uncertainties ahead.

Traditions and Cultural Diversity

The Spring

In Spring the horseman drives his plough
And lays his furrows row by row;
Like ripples of a rising tide
Across the arable they ride -
Then crooms to kill the tares and weeds,
With drills to sow the swelling seeds.
And some will fall and never grow,
Snatched straightaway by rook or crow.
And some will fall on stony ground;
So rootless, withered will be found
In the sun's blaze. And some will choke
'Mid thistle, devil's claw and dock.
And some will gleam with harvest gold
An hundred and an hundred fold,
Just as two thousand years ago
The Son of Man foretold it so.

A PRAYER

O God, we give you thanks for the world and all your good gifts, for our homes and our friends. As we celebrate the reawakening of the earth in spring, help us to face the future with hope and a determination to do our best.

Amen.

Traditions and Cultural Diversity

8

The Earth and Creation

Creation

* The 'Big Bang' theory of the origin of the universe
* The story of creation in Genesis
* Similarities between the two versions
* Order and logic in the universe
* The splendour of nature

The use of two contrasting pieces of music would enhance this assembly. At the beginning the theme music from the film '2001 – A Space Odyssey' could be used, and, at the end, the chorus 'The Heavens are telling the glory of God' from Haydn's 'Creation' would be suitable. The readings could be read by two different people. For a shorter assembly the readings could be summarized rather than read out in full.

A few years ago, scientists became very excited at new discoveries which, they believed, confirmed what is called the 'Big Bang' theory of the creation of the universe, and added considerably to the understanding of the evolution of the universe. One newspaper carried a huge headline across the front page which said, 'How the Universe Began'. Below were the words: 'A NASA spacecraft has detected echoes of the galaxies' birth fourteen thousand million years ago. The discovery about the formation of the universe after Big Bang has been hailed by scientists as the Holy Grail of cosmology.'

The Earth and Creation

The Big Bang concept states that, originally, all matter and energy were condensed to a single superdense point. About 15 billion years ago, there was a cataclysmic explosion resulting in an enormous release of heat and matter being hurled in all directions. All this took place in less than a second, but, since then, as the fragments have slowed down and cooled down, galaxies and stars have been formed. The process has continued, and the universe is still expanding. The newspaper article attempted to explain how information from the NASA spacecraft had added to the understanding of the process. The word 'Cosmos' is used to describe the universe as an ordered system. This is part of what the article said:

Fourteen thousand million years ago the universe hiccuped. Yesterday, American scientists announced that they have heard the echo.

A NASA spacecraft has detected ripples at the edge of the Cosmos which are the fossilised imprint of the birth of the stars and galaxies around us today. According to a leading British cosmologist, 'What we are seeing here is the moment when the structures we are part of – the stars and galaxies of the Universe – first began to form'. The ripples were spotted by the Cosmic Background Explorer (Cobe) satellite, and presented to excited astronomers at a meeting of the American Physical Society in Washington.

Cobe has provided the answer to a question that has baffled scientists in their attempts to understand the structure of the Cosmos. In the 1960s American scientists found definitive evidence that a Big Bang had started the whole thing off about 15 billion years ago. But the Big Bang would have spread matter like thin gruel evenly throughout the universe. The problem was to work out how the lumps (stars, planets and galaxies) got into the porridge ... Since the ripples were created almost 15 billion years ago, their radiation has been travelling towards Earth at the speed of light. By detecting the radiation, Cobe – 'a wonderful time machine' – is able to view the young universe ... Cobe has instruments on board which are sensitive to this extremely old radiation. The ripples Cobe has found are the first hard evidence of the long-sought lumpiness in the radiation ... 'The results show that the idea of a Big Bang model is once again brilliantly successful,' said a leading Professor.

(Extracts from *The Independent*, 24th April 1992)

Now here is part of the story of the creation of the world from the Book of Genesis in the Bible:

In the beginning of creation, when God made heaven and earth, the earth was without form and void, with darkness over the face of the abyss, and a mighty wind that swept over the surface of the waters. God said, 'Let there be light', and there was light; and God saw that the light was good, and he separated light from darkness. He called the light day, and the darkness night. So evening came, and the morning came, the first day.

God said, 'Let there be a vault between the waters, to separate water from water.' So God made the vault, and separated the water under the vault from the water above it, and so it was; and God called the vault heaven. Evening came, and morning came, a second day.

God said, 'Let the waters under heaven be gathered into one place, so that dry land may appear'; and so it was. God called the dry land earth, and the gathering of the waters he called seas; and God saw that it was good. Then God said, 'Let the earth produce fresh growth, let there be on the earth plants bearing seed, fruit-trees bearing fruit each with seed according to its kind.' So it was; the earth yielded fresh growth, plants bearing seed according to their kind and trees bearing fruit each with a seed according to its kind; and God saw that it was good. Evening came, and morning came, a third day.

(Genesis 1:1–13)

The account continues, following an ordered and methodical series of events, until: 'On the sixth day God completed all the work he had been doing, and on the seventh day he ceased from all his work.'

The newspaper article and the reading from Genesis give two very different versions of the creation of the universe, and, of course, they raise fundamental questions about the nature of the universe and the existence of God. In a short assembly it would be impossible even to attempt to answer those fundamental questions. Through discussion, reading and thought throughout our lives, we will probably all search for answers. But listening to those two very different accounts may help us to develop our thoughts. Two points, in particular, are worth noting.

The Earth and Creation

First, and perhaps surprisingly, there are a lot of similarities between the two stories. What scientists were trying to do was to find some explanation for the way things are in the universe. The discoveries of the satellite helped them to make their explanations more complete, and they were particularly excited because the new discoveries supported the Big Bang theory rather than contradicted it. The biblical story from Genesis is not believed by all Jews and Christians to be an attempt to describe what actually happened at the creation. Its main purpose is to show that everything comes from God, that everything fits together, and that there is harmony and goodness in everything. The similarities between the accounts are that they attempt to show that there is order and sense in the arrangement of things, and that everything does, indeed, fit together.

Secondly, everyone listening to the account of the mysteries of the universe, whether described by scientists or contained in the Bible, is filled with a sense of awe and wonder at the incredible splendour of nature. Whether we look at the universe from a religious or a scientific point of view, or both, or even from some other point of view, this sense of awe and wonder is almost overwhelming.

The scientific theory of the Big Bang may be a brilliant one (though not all scientists agree with it) but it poses an even more fundamental question, 'How and why did the Big Bang happen?' The whole concept of creation and the universe is, indeed, so awe-inspiring that many people feel there must be some supernatural power – some God – at work. Whatever our beliefs, let us think about the wonder of the universe, the splendour of nature, the glory of creation, and our own small but miraculous place in the order of things.

A PRAYER

O God, help us to see afresh the beauty that surrounds us, and
to take time to think about it in wonder and in awe.

Amen.

CHALLENGES FOR LIVING

The Celebration of Harvest

The Earth and Creation

* Ancient tradition of harvest festival
* Working creatively with nature
* Dangers of misuse of the world's resources
* Harvest as a celebration of achievement

Music would be a particularly appropriate addition to this assembly. One or more of the familiar harvest hymns could be sung or played, and perhaps John Betjeman's version of 'We plough the fields and scatter' could be sung as a solo. Parts of Beethoven's Sixth Symphony (the 'Pastoral') would make a suitable conclusion to convey the atmosphere of the countryside; the third movement pictures a festive group of country people, with the bassoon bringing out a note of rustic humour.

In Britain, only about two people in every hundred are directly engaged in the production of food; in other words, not many people work in farming. In the past, the proportion of the population working on farms was very much higher, and it is still much higher in many other countries. In Britain today, farming is a highly efficient business using a great deal of machinery. Large amounts of food are produced by relatively few people. It is therefore perhaps surprising that harvest festivals are so popular. But in churches, schools and elsewhere, people gather together for services, meals and celebrations. They bring food and flowers which are often distributed to those in need after the celebrations are over.

Why do harvest festivals command such support in a country where few work on the land and many people may go for months without seeing a cow or a cornfield?

Harvest is an ancient festival. It is much older than the Christian faith, indeed it is older than all the great religions of the world. It is old precisely because of its importance. A celebration connected with food must be one of the most fundamental of feasts, for without food we

143

The Earth and Creation

cannot survive. Ancient people knew this well, and that is why they observed harvest as a religious occasion.

In the harvest we see the human race using nature to obtain food for its needs. Humankind is bringing its energy to bear upon the world of nature. That is surely what human beings should be doing all the time, not just at the food harvest. By the operation of our creative minds and limbs, we should be working constantly to make best use of the natural world. So, in a sense, all the year is the harvest because in every day and month men and women act creatively upon the raw material of the world.

But as well as being a celebration of the natural world, harvest is a useful time to remind ourselves that we can all too easily misuse nature's resources. Far too often we care too little for nature. At a simple but important level, so many places are spoiled by litter and rubbish left either carelessly or deliberately by people who have not considered what the consequences would be if everyone behaved in a similar selfish manner. At another level, the exploitation of nature for greed and short-term gain is equally selfish and may well ruin the delicate balance of the earth's resources for future generations. In a humorous but telling way, John Betjeman wrote some alternative words to a well-known harvest hymn. There is much in his words to make us think.

We spray the fields and scatter
The poison on the ground
So that no wicked flowers
Upon the farm be found.
We like whatever helps us
To line our purse with pence;
The twenty-four hour broiler-house
And neat electric fence.

(John Betjeman, 'Harvest Hymn')

At harvest festival, then, we celebrate the abundance of nature and our use of the earth's resources to provide the food for our needs. Farmers have brought their energy to bear upon the world of nature. We think also of the misuse of nature – often caused by greed – and the vital necessity of conserving the natural world. But perhaps most of all we need to remember that human beings, at their best, can be creative all the time. We enjoy harvest festivals because we enjoy celebrating. On the surface, we are celebrating the successful gathering of food, but, at a deeper level, we need to celebrate all that is good, and all that we achieve. We should be using our minds, our skills and our talents to create a harvest every day.

A PRAYER

O God, we thank you for all the resources of the world and for life itself. Help us to work diligently and successfully together so that we may celebrate the harvest of life every day.

Amen.

Beauty and Pollution

✳ Variety of the earth in landscapes and seasons
✳ The equinoxes and the earth's orbit round the sun
✳ The beauty of spring
✳ Humankind's destruction of beauty – litter and other forms of pollution

This assembly is best timed to coincide with the spring equinox. Music from Vivaldi's 'Four Seasons' would be a suitable introduction. A large globe – able to spin at the correct angle – would be a useful visual aid. For a smaller gathering, the room could be darkened and a beam of light from a projector bulb could be trained on to the globe. A display of spring flowers alongside a collection of litter would help to highlight the theme.

The Earth and Creation

The world is amazingly varied – from the frozen wastes of Antarctica to the rainforests of Brazil, from the hot deserts of the Sahara to the lush green grass of Ireland, from the Himalayan peaks to the flat pampas of Argentina, from restful tropical beaches to the mighty force of Niagara Falls. There is so much variety that endless examples could be given. The seasons also are varied – from the cold of winter to the summer heat, from spring flowers to the golden colours of autumn, from the short daylight hours of midwinter to the long days of midsummer.

But despite all this diversity, on two days in the year everyone on earth has one important thing in common. Twice a year, everywhere in the world, the sun rises at 6 a.m. and sets at 6 p.m. – in Britain, in Australia, in Mexico, in Ethiopia, in Singapore, at the equator and in the tropics, in the Arctic and the Antarctic – everywhere, in fact. These days are called the equinoxes and they occur around 21st March and 21st September. In the northern hemisphere the first is called the spring equinox and the second the autumn equinox. Of course, in the southern hemisphere spring and autumn are the other way round.

Everyone knows that the earth completes its orbit around the sun in a year: that's what a year is – the time it takes the earth to go around the sun. As it goes round the sun, the earth is spinning. It spins round once every 24 hours: that's our day. Because it spins round, some of the time we are facing the sun – daytime – and some of the time we cannot see the sun – night-time. If the earth was not spinning, some places would have only continuous daytime or night-time.

However, as it spins, the earth is tilted: it spins at an angle compared with its rotation around the sun. Its axis is tilted 23½° from the horizontal. This means that at some times in the year each place is turned more towards the sun, and at other times in the year each place is turned more away from the sun.

The effect of all this is to give us our seasons – summer and longer days when we are tilted towards the sun, winter and shorter days when we are tilted away from the sun. The further you are from the equator, the greater the differences. At the equator there is little difference in the length of daylight and the seasons are very similar. But at the poles there is no darkness at all in midsummer and no light at all in midwinter. However, twice a year, at the beginning and the middle of the earth's orbit around the sun, come the equinoxes when the whole world is equal. In this country, the spring equinox marks the dividing line between the dark days of winter and the light days of summer.

One of the earliest signs of spring is the appearance of spring flowers. Very early in the year, before the equinox, come the aconites and snowdrops; then come the crocuses with their variety of colours. After that, the sight of thousands of daffodils is one of the great joys of spring and a sure sign that the dark days of winter are behind and that warmer weather is at hand.

Spring flowers are a reminder of the beauty of the world and the new life that comes with spring. Many people believe that God created such a varied and beautiful world for us to enjoy. But too often humankind seems to want to destroy the natural beauty of the world. Sometimes our destruction takes a dramatic form, such as the pollution of rivers or the atmosphere, or the construction of ugly buildings; sometimes it is less dramatic, but equally objectionable. We should do everything within our power or influence to prevent the destruction of the beauty of the world, and this needs to start with those things that every one of us can control directly. Perhaps an obvious example of this is the spoiling of the world by those who drop litter. People who pollute the beauty of the world by dropping litter are guilty of the same anti-social behaviour towards the environment as industries and governments that, on a larger scale, allow the destruction of the earth's beauty.

It is right to campaign against the major polluters of our planet and to recognize that what happens in one part of the world may affect people everywhere. But we need to do this sure in the knowledge that we have played our own part to prevent pollution in those areas directly within our control. A resolution not to drop litter and to do everything possible to keep the environment as pleasant, attractive and litter-free as possible, is an excellent objective to aim for in springtime. Of course, this ought to be an objective all the time in all our various environments – school, home, town and countryside; but in spring, when new life and fresh beauty surround us, it is particularly appropriate. So, let us think about the beauty of spring flowers and the beauty of the earth, and endeavour to play our part in getting rid of the ugly and enhancing the beautiful.

The Earth and Creation

The Earth and Creation

A PRAYER

O God, we give thanks for all the joys of springtime – the flowers that bring fresh colour into the world after the bleakness of winter, and the new life being born into the animal world. Keep us mindful of the joys of creation and help us to appreciate the beauty of the world.

Amen.

The Earth's Resources

✳ The 'fragility' of the earth
✳ The need to use resources wisely and fairly
✳ Comparing the earth to an item of clothing – creation, appropriate use, care, recycling
✳ Recycling as a means of conservation

A 'visual aid' of a jacket (or similar item of clothing), a number of years old, with a large interior label is needed if this section is used without modification. A poster showing a photograph of the earth taken from space would tie in with the opening paragraph and help to illustrate the theme of this assembly.

Nearly all the people who have had the privilege of travelling in space have said how beautiful the earth looks when seen from space. One of the astronauts who travelled to the moon said that if he could use only one word to describe the earth as seen from the moon, he would use the word 'fragile'. On its surface the earth seems solid enough, but from space it seemed so smooth and delicate and, above all, it seemed so fragile. It led him to recognize that the difference between the beautiful blue and white planet he could see from space and a black and brown one was very finely balanced. Was this beauty masking a senseless ugliness below? He realized how important it is to use the earth's resources wisely and that this should be our goal in our struggle to avoid ruining the planet.

To help us think about our world and the way we use it, a jacket can serve as an illustration. It is something that has been created; it has been well made and has been used for many years. So it is with our world: it has been created by a supernatural force – a force which many people call God; it was created many years ago and was well made. If we want to find out more about the jacket, we need to look at the label which will tell us various things about it. It says who created the jacket. It also gives details of the materials used – in this case wool and polyester. That reminds us about the world and its resources. Wool is a renewable resource: sheep can grow more wool. Polyester comes from oil which is a resource that is being rapidly used up. Oil takes millions of years to form deep below the surface of the earth, but, once used, it is gone very quickly.

What else is on the label? The size is an important piece of information. Different sizes are needed; it is no good if everything is the same. Similarly with the world: we need to get things right, and in the right proportions and amounts. But this is where we often seem to fail. In some parts of the world, there is too much – politicians speak of grain surpluses, butter mountains, wine lakes. Yet, in other areas, there is great hunger and poverty. There is an urgent need to get the world's balance right.

The label has further vital information. It gives instructions on how to look after the jacket and how to clean it. It would be disastrous to boil a garment that needs dry cleaning. The jacket can easily be ruined if it is not looked after properly. So it is with the world. It has been created for us to use, but we can ruin it if we don't look after it properly – if we pollute it, fight wars on it or mistreat it in other ways.

The example of the jacket simply illustrates the necessity to use the world's resources properly so that we can continue to enjoy the enormous variety of both renewable and non-renewable reserves, and so that the wealth of the world is not exhausted. We must strive to see that the world's resources are sensibly divided across the continents so that some parts do not get too much (too many large sizes, to use the example of the jacket), and other parts do not get too little (too many

The Earth and Creation

The Earth and Creation

small sizes). It is equally important that we look after the world properly so that it is a fit place for future generations. This places an enormous responsibility on the present generation of young people, and presents a very great challenge to them to make the world a better place in the future than it is today. Meeting this challenge will require co-operation across the world on a scale never seen before, but much can also be done at a local level anywhere in the world.

Recycling is part of the overall movement to care for our world and its resources. It is part of putting conservation above profit, and it is an essential element in the intelligent care of our precious and fragile planet. So when the jacket has completed its useful role as an item of clothing, it will not just be discarded and thrown away – it will be recycled and used in other ways. A thoughtful and creative view of what many would regard as litter, rubbish or waste is a very positive step towards a global strategy that conserves and preserves our fragile earth for future generations.

A PRAYER

✿

O God, give us a vision and a commitment to respect the earth which sustains us, rather than to waste and destroy it. Help us to value all living things while we have them, rather than finding too late that they have become extinct.

Amen.

Leap Years
and the Mysteries of Time

✳ The solar year and the calendar year
✳ The size and incomprehensibility of space
✳ The mysteries of life and of God

This assembly would be very appropriate for 29th February!
But, of course, it can be used in any year, particularly in
late February or early March. The hymn that is quoted
towards the end could be sung or a recording of it played.

t must be very hard to have a birthday on February 29th! As
everyone knows, this day occurs only once every four years, so
anyone born on 29th February has a birthday only every four years. A
year whose number is divisable by four is a leap year. So 1992, 1996,
2000, 2004 and so on are all leap years.

'Leap year' seems a strange name for a year that has an extra day. If
you leap over something, you are usually going fast and missing
something out, but in a leap year there is an extra day. The name may
come from the fact that in this year festivals and other events 'leap'
over a day: for example, if your birthday is on a Monday in 1999, it will
be on a Wednesday in 2000.

Leap years are necessary to offset the difference between the solar
year and the calendar year. The solar year is the time the earth takes to
make one orbit around the sun. That is 365.2422 days. The calendar
year, of course, is 365 days. To make up for the extra length of a solar
year, we have to add an extra day to the calendar year every fourth year.
But, no doubt you have worked out already that that isn't exactly right.
The solar year would have to be 365.25 days, not 365.2422 days, to
make things fit exactly. So, very occasionally, a leap year is missed out.
It is missed out in those centenary years whose numbers are not
divisible by 400. Therefore, 1900 was not a leap year. There's no need
to worry about remembering all the details because the next time a leap

year is missed will be 2100 and it's unlikely that many of us will still be around then! Perhaps some of you would like to work out how accurate this arrangement of the calendar is, and how many hundreds or thousands of years will pass before scientists and mathematicians decide that another adjustment is necessary.

Facts like this about the earth and the solar system are fascinating, but we need to remember that our earth and sun are just tiny parts of the universe. Facts about the size of the universe are staggering and virtually incomprehensible. The light of a star that we look at in the sky may have left that star thousands of years ago. Since all stars are moving at vast speed, the star is not, therefore, where it appears to be. It is indeed difficult to understand these things. If somehow we could be transported to a distant part of the universe in next to no time and could then look back at the earth through an extremely powerful telescope, perhaps we might see ourselves being born!

Travelling in time has, of course, long been a common feature of many science fiction books, but the idea helps to demonstrate the enormous mystery of the universe and the incredible miracle of life. None of us has any more than a tiny understanding of these amazing things. For many people, a belief in a supreme God is the inevitable consequence of any attempt to appreciate the wonder of the universe and the creation of life.

We need to strive to make good use of the privilege of life and perhaps it is appropriate to reflect on the wonders of the universe when we think of the reasons for having leap years. We may feel sorry for those whose birthdays occur on 29th February, but the arrangement of the calendar is one tiny example of humankind bringing its understanding of part of the universe to life here on our earth.

An eighteenth-century hymn writer explored the idea of an all-powerful and wonderful God in a hymn that is still well known. Here are the first two verses:

God moves in a mysterious way
His wonders to perform;
He plants his footsteps in the sea,
And rides upon the storm.

Deep in unfathomable mines
Of never-failing skill,
He treasures up His bright designs,
And works His sovereign will.

A PRAYER

O God, the creator of the universe, we ask for your guidance so that we may use the wonders of this world for the greater fulfilment of every person and every thing that is upon the earth.

Amen.

Space Travel

✳ Exploration of space and missions to the moon
✳ Human achievement in the Apollo project
✳ The importance of teamwork
✳ Immensity and wonder of the universe and creation
✳ Uniqueness of each human life

Posters showing photographs of the moon, and pictures of planets in orbit, stars in galaxies and so on, would help to illustrate the wonder of the universe. Some way of comparing the size of the Vehicle Assembly Building at Cape Canaveral with something within the experience of the pupils would be helpful; it is, however, difficult to find a meaningful example within direct human experience of the approximate 6 million million miles or 10 million million kilometres from our solar system to the nearest star!

The Earth and Creation

One of the most remarkable achievements of the human race in the past thirty years or so has been the exploration of space. From relatively modest beginnings with unmanned spacecraft circling the earth, to present-day projects to explore the outer planets of Jupiter, Uranus and Neptune, we have learned a lot about the solar system and beyond, and have marvelled at the wonders of space. Between 1969 and 1972 there were the stupendous achievements when men went to the moon, explored its surface and then returned to earth.

On 16th July 1969, the Apollo 11 spacecraft was launched into space by a giant Saturn V rocket to begin its journey to the moon. Four days later, on 20th July, the Eagle module carrying two astronauts from Apollo 11 landed on the surface of the moon. Neil Armstrong announced that the Eagle had landed, and subsequently the astronauts stepped out on to the surface of the moon, taking 'one giant leap for mankind'.

Between July 1969 and December 1972, six Apollo spacecraft went to the moon, and twelve human beings have walked on the surface of the moon. It was President Kennedy who, in 1962, made the declaration that it was the ambition of the United States to send people to the moon and bring them back safely, and that this ambition would be reached by the end of the decade. In fact, it was achieved with just five months to spare.

Many have argued that the enormous cost of the moon programme was not justified, but, whatever your views, the achievement of sending people to the moon and back is an enormous one and it illustrates dramatically what the human race is capable of doing if it really wants to. The skill, dedication and inventiveness of everyone involved demonstrates the heights to which the human race can ascend. It also underlines the value of teamwork. Only three people went into space on each mission and only two of them landed on the moon, but to get them there involved thousands and thousands of people. Designers, engineers, astronomers, computer operators, scientists and many, many more, all working together, enabled the project to be successful. Each one was as important as the others.

One of the favourite holiday destinations in the United States is Florida, with attractions such as Miami, the Everglades National Park and, of course, the Orlando area which includes Disneyland. Another place to spend an enthralling day, and only an hour's drive from

Orlando, is the Kennedy Space Center at Cape Canaveral on the Florida coast. It was from here that the Apollo spacecraft were launched to the moon, and where the present Shuttle space programme is based. The sheer size of the place is staggering. For example, the Vehicle Assembly Building, where the lunar projects were prepared, is 160 metres high, 218 metres long and 180 metres wide. Near this building is a Saturn V rocket – one that was not used because there was not enough money left at the end of the project. Its size is almost unbelievably vast, but this was necessary in order to blast the spacecraft successfully towards the moon.

However, if sending people to the moon demonstrates what the human race can do, it also highlights the immensity and the incomprehensible wonder of the universe. Perhaps the most spectacular achievement of humankind has been for twelve people to reach the moon. But in spite of the scale of the space programme, its complexity and its cost, once the spacecraft was out in space, it was insignificantly small. More than that, it went to the moon which is a small satellite of a small planet, the earth. The earth is one of nine planets associated with a small star which we call the sun. The sun is one of millions of stars which make up the galaxy known as the Milky Way. Beyond the Milky Way are countless other galaxies, each with millions of stars. It takes light more than four years to reach us from the nearest star, and light that we can see from other stars left those stars thousands of years ago.

It would be easy to produce many more mind-boggling statistics, but surely the point is made. Our world is a tiny part of the total universe, and our understanding of the universe is insignificant. We can only wonder at the awesome magnificence of creation. When many people contemplate the universe and creation, it reinforces their belief in a supernatural power – what they call God.

Contemplating the universe and creation could be depressing if all it did was to emphasize how insignificant each individual is. But it need not be depressing. It is equally awe-inspiring to consider the amazing diversity of life even in a small part of our world, and the uniqueness of every single human life. We all have our part to play. If that were not so, why were we created? The American moon project revealed how much can be achieved when people work together for a single purpose. But in our day-to-day lives we all have a unique role as individuals and as part of our society. Our uniqueness is as wonderful as the vastness of space.

A PRAYER

O God, as we contemplate the vastness of the universe and our unique position in it, help us to aim at achievements that are worth pursuing. Give us single-mindedness and energy to do our best so that we rise above the second-rate and contribute to the well-being of all people.

Amen.

Technology: the Forth Bridges

❋ Links between the natural world and the human world
❋ Humankind's creativity in solving problems
❋ Fitting technology to the natural world
❋ Positive and negative use of technology
❋ The challenge of making the right decisions

If possible, posters of the Forth Bridges would help to illustrate the points made in this assembly. Other pictures showing good examples of manmade technology harmonizing with the natural environment would be equally suitable.

The capital of Scotland is Edinburgh, and just to the north of Edinburgh is a large inlet of the sea which is the mouth – or Firth (to use the Scottish word) – of the River Forth. This wide expanse of water is also very deep and stretches a long way inland. For centuries it was a considerable obstacle to communications between the capital and the country to the north. Now, however, spanning the River Forth at Queensferry are two huge bridges, each one a masterpiece of engineering.

The older bridge, the Forth Railway Bridge, was opened over a hundred years ago in 1890. At the time it was opened it was the largest bridge in the world. It is no longer the largest, but it is still very impressive and is an example of what is called a cantilever bridge. Benjamin Baker, the designer, had the difficult task of designing a bridge to carry the railway across the wide, deep river, high enough to allow large ships to pass underneath. To do this he designed steel towers, each 105 metres high, one near each shore and one on an island in the river. From these a steel framework was built from shore to shore, using 50,000 tonnes of steel. The result was an impressive and very large bridge. The size is striking when you cross the bridge, or, if you see a train on the bridge, it looks tiny compared to the huge structure.

For many years after the building of the railway bridge, all other traffic had to continue to cross the river by ferry until the new Forth road bridge was built. The building of the road bridge was begun in November 1958 and the bridge was opened in 1964. It is an example of a suspension bridge, with a tall tower on either shore. The bridge is 2.5 kilometres long and, at the time of its building, was the largest suspension bridge in Europe.

The two bridges stand side by side. One is a tribute on a massive scale to late-Victorian engineering; the other is a graceful display of twentieth-century design and engineering. Both illustrate some important points about the relationship of humankind to our world.

First, it is possible for the made world to fit into the natural world. The area around the Forth bridges is very scenic and could have been ruined by these huge constructions. The railway bridge did, indeed, cause considerable controversy when it was built, but it is impossible not to admire the boldness of the design concept and, despite its massive scale, its balance in visual terms. The road bridge – so very different – is also appropriate in its setting. The two bridges show, within a splendid natural environment, human creativity at its best.

Secondly, the two bridges illustrate how the same design problem can have totally different solutions, both equally effective. The problem of bridging at a high level a wide deep inlet of the sea has been solved in two very different ways, both of which show human creativity at its best.

On a smaller scale, in our own lives, we can apply the same two points. First, our made world – our Technology – should fit in with the natural world, so that it complements nature, and does not destroy, harm,

The Earth and Creation

The Earth and Creation

desecrate or pollute it in any way. Secondly, we should use our creativity in all sorts of different ways for the benefit of the world. We are ingenious creatures, capable of bringing all kinds of solutions to all sorts of problems. We need to make sure that we use this creativity in a positive way.

Modern technology presents great challenges to all of us today. There are few things which technology cannot achieve, for good or ill. Ultimately, of course, the human race is capable of destroying itself and the world through the use of nuclear weapons. But in everything, from the disposal of crisp packets to the use of nuclear weapons, technology can be used positively or negatively. Almost all the activities of the human race have some effect on the world. A beautiful building enhances our environment, but an ugly one spoils it. Modern transport opens up endless possibilities for travel and recreation, but traffic pollution and insensitive new road schemes can harm and even destroy the environment. Technology – the made world – is everywhere. Modern education rightly stresses the importance of analysing problems, looking for possible solutions, and then implementing the one that best fits the situation. Making the right decision is the challenge to us all.

The designs of the two Forth bridges show responses that are appropriate both to the problem of communications between Edinburgh and the north of Scotland and to the splendour of the geographical setting of the Firth of Forth. In the story of the creation in the Bible, one phrase is repeated after each stage in the account: 'And God saw that it was good.' The world is, indeed, a wonderful place. We must make certain that it remains so. Our memorial must be to ensure that our technology complements and enhances the natural wonders of the world.

A PRAYER

O God, we give thanks for the natural wonders of our world and for all those manmade wonders which have been so useful to so many people. May our endeavours continue to enhance the miracle of creation for the benefit of all.

Amen.

Index of Themes

The page numbers are those of the first page of the relevant assembly, irrespective of where and how frequently the reference occurs within the assembly.

Index